IDEOLOGICAL INNOVATION UNDER MONARCHY

COMPARATIVE ASIAN STUDIES

Editors: Frans Hüsken and Dick Kooiman
Assistant executive editor: José Komen, Centre for Asian Studies Amsterdam

Publications in this series:

1. CONCEPTUALIZING DEVELOPMENT: The Historical-Sociological Tradition in Dutch Non-Western Sociology / Otto van den Muyzenberg and Willem Wolters / isbn 90-6765-382-9   39 pages ppb.

2. THE SHATTERED IMAGE: Construction and Deconstruction of the Village in Colonial Asia / Jan Breman / isbn 90-6765-383-7   50 pages ppb.

3. SEDUCTIVE MIRAGE: The Search for the Village Community in Southeast Asia / Jeremy Kemp / isbn 90-6765-384-5   47 pages ppb.

4. BETWEEN SOVEREIGN DOMAIN AND SERVILE TENURE: The Development of Rights to Land in Java, 1780-1870 / Peter Boomgaard / isbn 90-6256-788-6   61 pages ppb.

5. LABOUR MIGRATION AND RURAL TRANSFORMATION IN COLONIAL ASIA / Jan Breman / isbn 90-6256-873-4   82 pages ppb.

6. LIVING IN DELI: Its Society as Imaged in Colonial Fiction / Lily E. Clerkx and Wim F. Wertheim / isbn 90-6256-965-X   126 pages ppb.

7. STATE, VILLAGE, AND RITUAL IN BALI: A Historical Perspective / Henk Schulte Nordholt / isbn 90-5383-023-5   58 pages ppb.

8. THE CENTRALITY OF CENTRAL ASIA / Andre Gunder Frank / isbn 90-5383-079-0   68 pages ppb.

9. IDEOLOGICAL INNOVATION UNDER MONARCHY: Aspects of legitimation activity in contemporary Brunei / G. Braighlinn / isbn 90-5383-091-X   112 pages ppb.

CENTRE FOR ASIAN STUDIES AMSTERDAM

G. Braighlinn

Ideological Innovation under Monarchy

Aspects of Legitimation Activity in
Contemporary Brunei

VU University Press
Amsterdam, 1992

VU University Press is an imprint of:
VU Boekhandel/Uitgeverij bv
De Boelelaan 1105
1081 HV Amsterdam
The Netherlands

Lay-out by: Avo-text, Amstelveen
Printed by: Offsetdrukkerij Haveka bv, Alblasserdam

ISBN 90-5383-091-X CIP
NUGI 653

Contents

I. *Preface*

The type of political economy which combines a foundation of 'oil wealth' with autocratic Muslim monarchy as its State structure is by no means unique on the modern international scene, but the micro-state of Brunei Darussalam, based in two enclaves on the northern coast of Borneo and counting a mere 226,000 inhabitants (including about 52,000 transients), is the only example in the Malay world.

Brunei also happens to be enclosed by territories and territorial waters of eastern Malaysia. Owing to such close proximity, its indigenous population is constantly exposed, by way of Malaysian newspapers and television in the common national language, Malay, to the ideas of Malay democratic nationalism. Moreover, in 1963 Brunei itself came within a trice of incorporation into the Federation of Malaysia.

The sultanate is thus not just unique in regional political terms, but its present territorial existence has some features of an accidental phenomenon as well. It is not unlikely that a State or polity of this kind, in all these circumstances, would perceive a strong imperative to rationalise and justify its existence to its subjects.[1]

Ironically enough, the Malaysia merger negotiations were conducted for Brunei by the late Sultan Omar Ali Saifuddin III - the very ruler who would subsequently elaborate the foundations of the neo-traditional polity between his own formal abdication in 1967 and full independence from Britain in 1984. Perhaps acquaintance with the Malaysian model gave the sultan insight into its potential attractions for his own people and its disadvantages in other respects, and helped to suggest some conditions for the revival of monarchical government in a contrastive regional environment.

Be that as it may, ideological propagation is certainly a lively concern of the present administration, that of Sultan Hassanal Bolkiah. Its many-sided product is as audible as it is visible, and easy enough to document. While its effects are necessarily more a matter for speculation or, at best, impressionistic sociological jottings, one need have no doubt that a perceived need to counter the appeals of alternative, exogenous models - above all, the Malaysian example - weighs heavily among the motivating factors or 'causal dynamics' of the said propagation.

For the observer inclined towards social science theory and analysis, the Brunei case will be likely to constitute a stimulating example with reference to the role of created ideas in changing power relationships or confirming them. At a time of rapid socio-economic change, ideas might play a more vital role than the 'social structure' and 'culture' which may have featured in our assumptions as the more manifest, almost defining bearer and diffuse agent, respectively, of major political transformation as well as fundamental continuity. But it is far too early to try to prove the validity of such a premise, and the attempt will not be made. All that can be said with certainty is that the ideologues themselves set great store by the efficacy of ideas. The primary aim of the study is thus the quite modest one of presenting new information on a new subject - Brunei ruling-elite ideology - ordered as meaningfully as possible by the different 'areas of reality' to which the ideologues address themselves, but with no intensive reference to social and political impact. The sociological projections which play down the role of ideas, in the final section, are extremely tentative.

Meanwhile, among the deeper considerations motivating the project, it would not be out of place to admit to a certain 'Verfremdung' in face of the diversionary adaptation of worthy scholarly traditions, such as historiography, to political purposes. A social scientist who was not well aware of such a phenomenon would be unworthy of his name, yet observations made at the interface with 'Herrschaft' may add an 'edge' to understanding, and help to rekindle old respect for Marx, with special reference to the dichotomy between ideologies of 'oppressed' interests, geared to social transformation, and ideologies of reactionary interests, geared to stabilisation and foisting 'false consciousness' upon their consumers. The typology may take on enhanced meaning for individuals having some familiarity with a political system which evinces elements of the former category, as does peninsular Malaysia.

The study was completed, at a diplomatic distance from the action, in the later months of 1991.

2

II. *Introduction: A Comparative Discussion*

West Malaysia, with its own characteristic Malay ideology, actually provides a useful comparative yardstick by which to evaluate or classify the Brunei case. For one thing, a comparison of Brunei and the nine peninsular Malay States in terms of their respective processes of decolonisation will help to clarify how a monarchical government, with the need and capacity to rationalise itself ideologically, was able to rise to its position of pre-eminence in the first place. (Much more on this in Section IV.) It goes without saying that we shall also need enough historical background on Brunei to assess historical claims of the State ideology where the objective background of the contemporary power structure seems to have been denied or distorted. The more important focus of comparison, however, occupying the rest of this section, will be on the contrasts between the ideologies of peninsular Malay nationalism and the Brunei ruling elite. Consideration of the former may serve to cast some initial heuristic light on the distinctively static assumptions of Brunei elite ideology about historical change in particular. (But again it will be relevant to bear in mind that a static ideological model may have the precise function of denying or distorting the extent to which the power structure is actually a product of significant sociological transformation.)

Right at the start of our comparison we will be struck by the fact that indigenous society in the peninsular States as well as in Brunei is predominantly Malay - and thus (by social definition in both places, and political definition too in West Malaysia) Muslim. Also, Brunei's exposure to peninsular Malay culture and political influence has been intensive throughout the 20th century. However, the striking dissimilarities of these polities at the present time include the purely constitutional status of the sultans of the nine peninsular Malay States and the rotating kingship of Malaysia, beside the absolute power of the sultan of Brunei; and the fact that the peninsular monarchies were only preserved in any form because of the Malay need for a symbol of racial supremacy in a territory that was swamped by Chinese and Indian immigration during colonial rule. Furthermore, and paradoxically, Malay nationalism is ambivalent towards its royal protectors, whose forebears 'presided' in some degree over those migrations both before and during Indirect Rule, did little to prepare Malay society to compete economically with the newcomers, and even signed away their sovereignty for a while to a centralising, racially egalitarian British colonial government in 1946. Whereas, across the water in Borneo, the Brunei monarchy vaunts the denial of citizenship to most Chinese, and indeed the relatively low levels of immigration during British protection, as achievements of royal government, which obviate any need for struggle. What royal government did not manage to prevent was the massive loss of empire, mainly to British interests in the 19th century, and thus to Malaysia itself by colonial succession in 1963. But popular attention can be diverted from that disaster, to a large extent, by the claim of successful protection of racial sovereignty in the territory that survives. Many Brunei Malays believe in the natural rapacity of all foreigners, and do not seem greatly inclined to blame their own rulers for historical losses.

Meanwhile, in West Malaysia the theme of struggle dominates Malay political discourse. The peninsular Malay ideology that is in question is not to be confused with the insipid statement of multi-racial goodwill known as the *Rukunegara*. This doctrine was designed in the early 1970s to patch over the rifts engendered, if not revealed, by the racial riots of 1969. Rather, what is of concern here is the dynamic ideology of ethnic self-assertion which, from the point of view of the non-Malay victims of 1969, was the very cause of the riots. Malay nationalism had tried to teach the peninsular Malays to see themselves as a beleaguered people, whom only democratic political organisation, racial unity, self-conscious economic pugnacity or entrepreneurial spirit, and control of the instruments of State power (preferably but not necessarily behind a screen of constitutional legitimacy) could first save from dispossession or extinction in their own land, then lead forward to a new age of supremacy.[2] To that list of prescribed attributes may perhaps be added, from the era of Dr Mahathir's ascendency, psychological independence and Islamic revival.[3]

It will be noted that all these attributes are relevant to the ongoing conduct of political economy in independent Malaysia, over and above the campaign which won a bloodless independence for Malaya (epic though it was in 1957). That the spirit of 'permanent revolution' which could lift a Dr Mahathir to the pinnacle of power has latterly become the vehicle and vindication of neo-monarchical pretensions and an incipient autocracy will not surprise any student of history.[4] Nor will the institutionalised manipulation of popular support through the mechanisms of a dominant party system

4

astonish any student of politics. Yet Dr Mahathir has continued to invoke his 'democratic' mandate: the unresolved problem of Malay economic backwardness as the twenty-year New Economic Policy comes to an end, and the ideology of struggle by the would-be oppressed. There are therefore, by implication, further, unfulfilled stages on the Malays' journey towards perfection. One might correspondingly suggest that there are unfulfilled steps in Dr Mahathir's own accumulation of power and personal succession to still functional, legitimating monarchical structures. Whatever Dr Mahathir's private aspirations, the time for a new dynasty and an end-of-history ideology is not yet. The absence of the latter in Malaysia is a feature distinguishing peninsular Malay nationalist attitudes from the general spirit of elite thinking and propagated belief in Brunei.[5]

At any rate, a realistic scenario for Malaysia is probably an ideology which somehow justifies the leader's power (while denying him absolute power) in terms of 'uncompleted tasks' or 'ever-lurking dangers', rather as Communist regimes have done. In other words, the ideology itself would not claim that history was truly 'at an end'. And we shall see that even the government of Brunei invokes some slight dangers and necessary national tasks in justification of absolutism. (Sometimes the government calls upon the people to actively fulfil the ideology as well as believe in it. Indeed! Why have an ideology if the reputed *status quo* or the 'natural order' are immune to all dangers?)[6] But this is not to the detriment of the basic 'end of history' posture in question. Indeed, in its reactionary guise or 'personality', in invoking historical legitimacy - almost in direct proportion to any objective novelty in its absolutism - the Brunei regime does not admit to any prior historical *process* of significance, either ancient or modern, that could have brought it to power either: it is perhaps 'above' historical process rather than at the 'end' of it. Historical process is played out basically on a world stage, in a drama in which Brunei scarcely rates a 'walk-on part' or is merely a spectator to!

It may not take a strongly Marxist frame of mind to detect more than a touch of 'false consciousness' here, projected to the Bruneian consumers of ideology by an established and actively self-consolidating elite. Whether or not a sociologist might conceive the Brunei masses as an 'oppressed group' in any sense, like the masses which feature in peninsular Malay ideology, it is clearly not the desire of their government that they should thus perceive themselves. If there has ever been an interest suffering 'oppression', it would have to be the royal interest itself, now happily liberated from colonial

5

tutelage. Least of all is there any room here for the peninsular view that royalty collaborated in some way with colonialism against the interests of the masses; nor for the notion that the supersession of royal power constitutes an uncompleted chapter of national history.

It remains but to add that to speak even predictively of an end-of-history *ideology* - if the 'end of history' be either objective or sincerely subjective - is to take a little distance from Marx in his own more ideological guise. In the imaginary event that Mahathir's neo-absolutism were to be consolidated, it should logically be accompanied by an ideology asserting that, in critical respects, ethnic inequality was overcome and struggle redundant, while by its very existence and assertions proving that some other sort of contradiction was alive and well; and this, overall, would approximate the kind of reactionary doctrine and political stratification currently characteristic of Brunei. At the same time it must again be stressed that while the Brunei polity in many ways invites characterisation as 'reactionary' (the late sultan did, after all, overthrow democracy), the ideological innovation which is the focus of this study has some connection with the novel aspects of this absolutist State. That is, not only is the sultanate without any contemporary analogue in the region, but there is no persuasive structural precedent in Brunei history itself before 1959. The very shrinkage of territory creates entirely novel possibilities of control.

Now to lay emphasis on novelty in State structures is hardly *de rigeur* in Southeast Asian Studies at the present time ('essential continuity' or at least 'old forms in new manifestations' are the current prescriptions, in reaction against 'Eurocentric' approaches); yet while a kind of stagnation may emerge as pervasive, and the State is positively laden with 'traditional ceremony', it does seem worthwhile to initially approach this absolutist system-that-is-set-to-stagnate in terms of its many novel traits, the product of a recent era. (Dr Mahathir aspires, but the Brunei monarchy acquires!) The author does not propose to present a methodical argument in favour of classifying even the Brunei royal family as a 'new class'; nor will he dwell on the possible irony that the rise of a 'nation'-state can go hand in hand with extreme stratification and a strategy for its consolidation (the study is not conceived as a contribution to sociological theory, and in any case, the manipulation of independence or struggles of national emancipation to advance one or another class interest is a sufficiently familiar phenomenon of this century); but if the reader will keep these perspectives in view, they may cast tentative illumination on some of the data at hand.

6

Apart from the fact that almost literal 'control of the means of production' makes the royal family a ruling class by classical definition, a 'new class' perspective is urged, initially, by the fact that the sultan acquires wealth by virtue and by means of his control of a newly independent modern State. Furthermore, he employs his wealth in order to constantly consolidate that control, and simultaneously utilises State institutions and the government apparatus to shroud both his financial and political dealings in secrecy. Above all, he eschews the search for any more durable polity which would preserve the prestige of the monarchy but at the same time disperse or diffuse control of national wealth. The aforesaid 'new class' perspective may also help to clarify the manifest *urgency* with which ideological tasks are addressed. Although in its origins a solidary status-group rather than a 'class', the royal family now operates in ways which are far more defined by economic imperatives. (Perhaps even the intensification of family endogamy by the 'architect of modern Brunei', the late sultan - in marrying both his eldest son and his eldest daughter to their first cousins despite known genetic risks - may be adduced in this connection.) The royalty are highly conscious of the transformation of their condition within the span of a lifetime. And while at present it is the influence of exogenous models on popular sentiment that most needs to be counteracted by ideological innovation, growing popular consciousness of class division and inequality will become the main necessitating factor in the event that the Brunei State proves unable or unwilling to continue policies of incremental welfare. If, lastly, the ruling interest were to combine ideological propagation with the building of supporting coalitions (with or without a clear class complexion at first, but characterised by self-interested solidarity with the sultan and his family in distinction to 'love of nation'), the 'new class' perspective would receive further validation. So, also, would the concept of contemporary, active socio-political process, already foreshadowed by the notion that State ideology stands in need of support or must be 'fulfilled', and amply confirmed by any creative flexibility in the writing of ideology that may come to light as time goes by.[7]

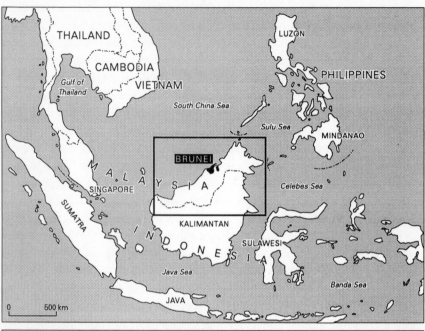

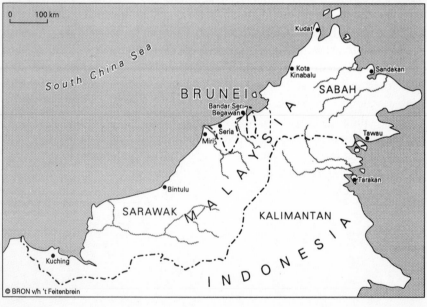

© BRON v/h 't Feitenbrein

III. *Overview*

At all events, it is perhaps high time to revert from comparative and theoretical reflection to a more descriptive mode. By and large, this study takes the form of a series of sketches of ideological output relating to various spheres of reality, with rather more emphasis on descriptions of the world than the prescriptive dimension (which to some extent the ideologues leave . implicit, possibly because what is described is a stratified model, mere conformity to which - if it exists - must be automatically 'stabilising'). Of course the author would like to link all the sketches into a coherent totality of 'legitimation activity', but in a situation where ideology is being generated by a number of different individuals, each according to his own sphere of interest or specialisation (probably with scant coordination among them, even if the terms of an overarching formula have emerged in the course of recurrent social contact), the account may seem at times a little *ad hoc*, like its own subject matter. There is a tentative, three-phased sociological conclusion relating to factors for rejection or endorsement of State ideology, but it cannot be considered to comprise more than a few 'pointers to further research'. Expressed in another way, the generation of ideology that we see today is almost as new as the emergent political structure which it serves. Thus it is as difficult to give a holistic account of it as it is to integrate it with the suggested, inchoate context of incipient 'contradiction' as well as complementary interest. In the words of a time-honoured (if not hoary) alibi, the author would beg to claim an essentially 'preliminary' status for the study.

The study will get properly under way, as previously mentioned, by examining, in Section IV, the historical circumstances of the rise of modern Brunei, with some continuing comparative reference to contemporary developments in Malaysia. Section V deals with the official and formal ideology known as 'M.I.B.', with some passing empirical comments on the sociological reality which the ideology purports to describe but may in fact be more concerned (at least on the whole) to mould in order that its hierarchical principles shall be fulfilled in practice. Section VI considers the ways in which the British Residency period - an embarrassing break in the historical continuity postulated by M.I.B. - is rationalised into insignificance. Then

Section VII looks at the uses of the ancient past in relation to regime legitimacy, after observing that the objective history of 20th-century nationalism is entirely dysfunctional to the interests of the present structure.

From here, we move to complementary developments in Islamic doctrine: first, an attempt to 'liberalise' the basic State ideology itself by postulating the existence of a social contract (Section VIII); secondly, the more 'mainstream', orthodox position of the Islamic establishment that there are no temporal limitations on a 'caliph' (Section X). The latter position is highly consistent, of course, with the static or non-processual propositions of M.I.B. But this will be the place to remark that Islamisation becomes vital in direct proportion to the liabilities of monarchy and dangers of nationalism as reference points for political legitimation in the Brunei context; and indeed any shift of emphasis within the ideology, one way or the other - intensified Islamisation is also a shift, not to say an important innovation - will tend to betray the fact that the real environment of the Brunei State, internal and external, is far from static and is capable of evoking ideological and/or policy responses (such as aggregative action) which react *upon* the environment in their turn: for example in the form of demands for behavioural convergence on the model - a singular case of the social and historical process which Bruneian doctrine denies. Also less than consonant with M.I.B. (with its hierarchy, basically, but also with the notion of 'unchanging essence' in society) are the participatory implications of national development strategy - though here a careful examination of official statements in themselves suggests that a degree of consistency has been achieved 'on paper' (see Section XI). Meanwhile, Section IX will have filled in some background on the cultivated image of the late sultan which is complementary to the 'caliphate' theory, but less so, paradoxically, to the idea of 'unchanging essence', as it involves a purported royal struggle for independence.

Only in the ideological construction of the international environment (Section XII) are historical change and process acknowledged; but ironically, as the Gulf War has helped to confirm, the analytical acknowledgement and even political support which the Brunei government has rendered, under the terms of its 'international world view', to Third World nationalist movements (especially Muslim nationalism) need not be expected to have any destabilising consequences for the existing Brunei structure. On the contrary, the regime may have calculated (and if so, rightly) that international Muslim issues can serve as a 'safety valve' for residual nationalist sentiment, rendering Kuwait an object of popular contempt or indifference for Brunei Malays yet with no corresponding tendency to notice parallels between the political economies, political structures and defence arrangements of Kuwait and Brunei (Section XIII).

The study moves towards a conclusion in Sections XIV and XV by discussing the prospects that certain groups might come to perceive ideology as an instrument of legitimation for the present ruling interest, and therefore as something to be at first discredited and disbelieved, then substituted by more objective analyses of Brunei's situation as well as a less elitist vision of the future. However, the reactions to the Gulf War among various Brunei strata may justify a different conclusion: that the capacity of Bruneians to absorb, accept and act upon authoritative political doctrine - the official ideological construction of political reality and its prescriptive corollaries - is more deeply rooted than foreign observers normally find it possible to conceive (Section XVI).

Alternatively, if the masses are, in reality, volatile, and their submission depends upon the skill of the ruling elite in designing and projecting doctrine, the demonstration of such skill could form the basis for a broader coalition of protective self-interest centred on the monarchy and the religious establishment. The prospect that ideology will realise its purposes - 'make the dream a reality', as it were - is thereby greatly strengthened. But what is perhaps most important, at a minimum, is neither that society should 'fulfil', or reify, the archaic or neo-traditional sociological forms postulated by ideology; nor truly respond to calls for, say, economic action, which imply a little change in the converse, 'other' direction (modernity); but rather, that it should deliver support to the regime simply by declaring loyalty to the official beliefs of the State. Always, *political support* is of the essence. Even if this were delivered in a basically symbolic way, by public acknowledgement in key quarters that M.I.B. represents moral and objective 'truth' - whatever people might privately believe and privately do - the regime would still have gained a worthwhile asset.

IV. *The Modern Brunei Polity*

The uniqueness of Brunei is highlighted at a mundane level by the fact that the sultanate entered the Commonwealth, upon recovering 'full independence' from Britain in January 1984, without the institution of a popular franchise, and within weeks had even abolished the nominated Legislative Assembly. This situation makes Brunei an 'odd man out' among the states of the Association of Southeast Asian Nations (ASEAN), to which it likewise acceded. Elections have been a basic mechanism of political legitimation for incumbent elites or ruling alliances not only in the four colonially created states of ASEAN (the Philippines, Indonesia and Singapore, as well as Malaysia) since their independence, but also in recent decades in the ancient kingdom of Thailand.[8] Certainly, elections are a shared norm of the five founder members of the association at the present time. In Brunei itself, for that matter, as in most other erstwhile British colonies and protectorates, independence has been commonly equated in popular thinking with the rise of political participation. These factors create an urgent need for the Brunei State to rationalise and justify neo-traditional political structure, mainly though not exclusively to its own subjects. It is the efforts in this direction that constitute, indeed, the essential point of focus of the present study.

Initially, however, it may be helpful to rehearse the steps by which Brunei contrived to 'emerge' as a fully independent state in this form. At this point the analysis will reach back only as far as the late 1950s, drawing further parallels as necessary with the Malay States.

In 1957 the nine Malay States and two former crown colonies of the peninsula gained their independence as the 'Federation of Malaya'. The process of emancipation had been somewhat accelerated by the sweeping success of the multi-racial Alliance coalition in the first general elections of 1955. No doubt, the moderation of the brand of Malay nationalism represented by Tunku Abdul Rahman, president of the United Malays National Organisation (UMNO), helped to make the hand-over more palatable to British interests. This Malay mass movement led by a progressive aristocracy had come into being to fight the radical, centralising and racially egalitarian Malayan Union Constitution of 1946. The nine State monarchies were duly preserved, in a federal and democratic framework (and with a rotating kingship since 1957), but as symbolic protectors of the Malays for the most part, with a few reserve powers. The true functional heir to British power and the Malays' more dynamic protector was to be a nationalist political party - with the significant ideological corollaries that have been mentioned above.

In Brunei, by contrast, no comparable issue activated the upper class to seek a popular political base - not even administrative subordination to Sarawak and the patent incapacity for national leadership of the inebriate Sultan Ahmad Tajuddin. When nationalism took hold on a mass basis it was thus instigated by a more radical party, the Brunei People's Party or *Parti Rakyat Brunei* (PRB). But by now the monarch in the person of Omar Ali Saifuddin III was developing pretensions to leadership in a highly conservative mould which anyway tended to open the way to more radical tendencies of mass political organisation. PRB's socialist inclination engendered incipient subjective polarisation in Brunei society along class lines. Both the British (though embarrassed by the sultan's anti-democratic views) and of course the sultan himself experienced some foreboding.[9] The PRB, for its part, withheld cooperation from tentative constitutional reforms on the grounds that they were not substantial enough.[10] The upshot of such disunity was that the 1959 Constitution gave self-government in advance of the formation of a democratic legislature and even before elections had been held to district councils. Constitutional caution was manifest in the procedure for constituting the future Legislative Council: only the four district councils would be directly elected; they in turn would nominate a total of sixteen popular representatives to the Legislative Council, but the sixteen would be outnumbered by eight *ex officio*, six official and three nominated members.[11] Even more significant was the fact that absolute power over State finances was vested in the sultan,[12] and that the executive council was not to be responsible to the legislature. Indeed the sultan was liberally exempted from the requirement to consult the executive council itself.[13] At this point the sultan's obduracy had paid off for him, and the PRB's refusal to cooperate had played into his hands.

On the most generous assumption, British decision-makers may have been anxious to launch Brunei on a path of constitutional development and decolonisation by 1959, however tentatively, so that the state should not fall too far behind Sarawak and Sabah in terms of socio-political development, or as a 'colonial anomaly' excite the animosity of Indonesia in due course.

To delay constitutional advance in any form would have been to deliver the political advantage to the 'demagogue', Azahari. It was really 'Hobson's choice'. But changes in the 1959 mould, not less radical, in a way, than in Malaya, may also seem a high price to have paid for just a little 'movement'. Could conflict be avoided between a ruler thus fortified and the future legislative branch?[14]

Elections took place one year behind schedule, in August 1962, giving the whole block of 16 indirectly elected seats to the PRB. The implacable hostility of the party to the idea of Brunei joining the proposed Federation of Malaysia (a 'merger' of the Federation of Malaya with Singapore, Sabah, Sarawak and Brunei), which Sultan Omar Ali Saifuddin was discussing in apparent earnest, goes some way towards explaining both the victory of the party and the reluctance of the government to convene the Legislative Council thereafter and countenance a hostile debate and resolution. In British eyes the federation proposal would have offered a new and possibly more promising prospect of nudging Brunei towards an independence combined with democracy.[15] But if the outlook seemed rosier in this framework than under the Brunei Constitution, at the same time a system of democracy and independence achieved through Malaysia might not favour the PRB. Obviously 'security' was one British motive behind the Malaysia plan, while PRB's more 'bourgeois' political rivals in Brunei had placed themselves in relationships of clientage to their Malayan counterparts, and were looking forward to high appointments in the new federation. Therefore PRB, however misguidedly, took the post-election manoeuvres as a sign that the British and their friends were determined to push Brunei into Malaysia at any cost. The party launched its ill-fated rebellion in December 1962. Thus was polarisation perfected - an ironical yet not entirely surprising outcome of a Constitution which legitimated the sultan's exclusive right to guide his country's destiny. There was not even a conflict between ruler and legislature as such, for the rebellion occurred in connection with the ruler's failure to convene it![16]

In retrospect, 1962 stands out as the seminal year in the consolidation of Brunei's modern monarchical system. The rebellion had started some months before Indonesia expected it or was in a position to support it under plans for confrontation against Malaysia. British forces from Singapore quickly got the upper hand over the rebels, the PRB was banned and the constitutional provision for elections abolished.[17] The British obliged the sultan by arresting a fugitive leader of PRB, Zaini Ahmad, in Hongkong and returning him to Brunei for detention with other captured rebels. In July 1963, however, the sultan decided to reject membership in Malaysia. The terms were unfavourable, especially with regard to oil. But there was also a lot more oil, offshore, than had previously been dreamed of, and this guarantee of Brunei's economic viability as a separate state was in turn guaranteed, like the monarchy itself, by a British Gurkha Battalion now stationed permanently in the oil field, guarding henceforth an Anglo-Bruneian asset. Still, any taste for radical politics had been shocked out of the population for some time to come by the trauma of the rebellion and its suppression.

The next year (1964), the sultan consented to a revival of democratic activity, but on a basis rather more restricted than in 1962, with only ten elected (albeit directly elected) members as against five nominated and six *ex officio*.[18] Following elections in March 1965, a legislature thus constituted met regularly in the second half of the 1960s. Despite considerable British pressure for a responsible cabinet, the sultan would only go as far as to appoint two 'assistant ministers' from the elected ranks of the 'Legco'.[19] The 1967 abdication of Sultan Omar Ali Saifuddin in favour of his eldest son, Hassanal Bolkiah, brought no interruption in the institution of a semi-elective legislature. But some observers have seen the abdication as a stratagem to avoid British pressure for complete democratisation and the termination of protection. (It certainly put paid to local manoeuvres directed towards the same ends and led by Brunei's last legal and serious political party, the *Barisan Kemerdekaan Rakyat* or 'BAKER'.) It does not therefore seem inconsistent that when the British Labour government was preparing, nothing daunted, to abrogate the 1959 Brunei Agreement (the treaty of protection) unilaterally, and leave Brunei in every sense to its own devices, the sultan turned the tables by promulgating a constitutional amendment to give effect to a far more 'customary' structure for the legislature than before, namely 6 *ex officio*, 5 official and 10 nominated members.[20]

In the event, British 'withdrawal east of Suez' was modified when the Conservatives won the 1970 election. The Brunei monarchy could now look forward to several more years of consolidation, free from the shadow of elections yet still 'shaded' by a protecting power. The incoming Heath Administration gave a respite to Brunei by the amended agreement of 1971 as regards foreign affairs and defence (though the basis of the latter commitment was henceforth consultative), in combination with optimum terms on the domestic side. Britain's residual formal right of advice in internal matters was renounced and internal security handed over to the Brunei government. Consistently with the termination of all internal responsibility, there was no interference with the legislative structure established in 1970. In fact, since 'external responsibility' was expressed most visibly by a strong military presence, surviving or reviving democratic forces were inclined to see Britain as a committed *supporter* of the legislative structure. But if their assessment was valid up to a point, the royal family was protected even more by the limitations of nationalist thinking itself, which completely failed to conceptualise the combination of executive power with self-enrichment, behind the British shield, as the development of a resilient class interest.

It remained only for Britain to withdraw from external responsibility in due course. The sultanate clung even more tenaciously to British protection in the mid-1970s, in face of a PRB revival supported by Malaysia. This support facilitated a dramatic escape of detainees (including Zaini Ahmad) and brought the case of Britain's 'refusal to grant self-determination' before the United Nations. But the Labour Administration of the late seventies was able to prevail upon Brunei to sign an independence agreement in 1979 (the Treaty of Friendship and Cooperation) after a change of regional posture in Malaysia. Unlike the case in 1970, the new Conservative Administration of Mrs Thatcher did not reverse Labour policy, which on this occasion was enshrined in a treaty, but in 1983 did extend the life of the secret 'Exchange of Letters' which governs the position of the Gurkha Battalion in Brunei both as to the terms of its commitment in case of need and its subsidisation by the sultan. In such a condition of both external and internal reassurance provided by a British Conservative government (whatever may be the precise content of the secret letters with regard to internally-based insurgency), the sultanate again acted consistently by suspending the whole of Parts VI and VII of the Constitution relating to the Legislative Council, less than three months after 'full independence'.[21] (The last meeting of the council had taken place in December 1983.) Legislation is now enacted either by the sultan under emergency powers or by the minister of justice under a Law Revision Act. The presence of the Gurkhas is one important psychological deterrent to opposition, but there are numerous other mechanisms of dominance and control. There are two further battalions of Gurkhas employed directly by the sultan to guard key installations, including the arsenal of the Royal Brunei Armed Forces. Currently, only one lame political party has a licence to exist and there is rigorous press and academic censorship.[22]

It is plain that while the sultanate welcomes British protection under whatever name, today no less than before 1984, it has not accepted that British political ideas need be part of the 'subscription' or necessary costs of the relationship. On the contrary, it has enjoyed some success in consolidating neo-traditional political structure even at times of British military intervention or guaranteed presence - and almost more so then than otherwise. Before 1979, British Labour governments were not able to insist on democracy as a condition of an independence which (in the absence of democracy) Britain, not Brunei itself, was demanding.[23] Both before and since 1984 the maintenance of a full Gurkha Battalion at the sultan's expense, and the balanced Anglo-Dutch/Bruneian stake in Brunei Shell Petroleum, have sealed a bond of mutual interest with Conservative governments which may partly explain their restraint in the matter of Brunei's long-term political prisoners, at least until Mrs Thatcher herself was put under pressure by Mr 'Tiny' Rowland in late 1989.[24]

Meanwhile, under the ASEAN principle of mutual non-interference, faithfully extended to the association's sixth member, Brunei finds its regional environment now considerably less threatening than during the Malaysian mini-confrontation of the 1970s. The sultanate takes some justifiable pride in its statecraft and has institutionalised a strong subjective sense of its moral autarchy today, free from alien political philosophies, and claims freedom from colonialism in the past, even during the era of the British Residency, 1906-59. Such assets will not defend themselves. But the power to defend them exists.

V. Overt Ideology

Since before independence, moral autarchy has been a standard theme in official communication with the Brunei public, and its purported manifestations have begun to be fairly methodically elaborated as a prescriptive system (for 'nation-building'), the more so as social reality currently falls short of the ideal in some respects. Indeed considerable faith seems to be placed in ideology as an instrument of mental 'structuring' of a population unpractised in political debate and analysis. Nor is it felt to be counter-productive to inform the people that it is an 'ideology' that they are being fed, as a normal complement to the life of a nation which needs to 'know its identity'. The epithet 'national ideology' is applied even more often to Islam separately than to the composite doctrine described below.

One incidental hint of the uncritical reception of authoritative intellectual outputs (if it is not that the authorities themselves are uncritically complacent) is found in the way the government has confidently advertised an exercise in persuading the *British* public of the legitimacy of the Anglo-Bruneian connection, for reading by *Bruneians*, in spite of contradictions between its condescending, Anglocentric platitudes and the tendency to nullify the British connection in official presentations in Malay.[25] In fact the image of an Anglicised and Anglophile sultan may not be remote from the way the sultan sees himself. Most members of the elite are proud of their cosmopolitan attributes and use English for preference. The interesting point is that contradictions in Bruneian public images and between disparate assertions of official ideology are not felt to carry penalties.

In considering the theme of self-legitimating efforts by the Brunei State directed specifically towards its own people, let us begin with the characterisation of the working socio-political system of Brunei as a 'Malay, Islamic monarchy'. This characterisation, so far as fulfilled in current reality, does not necessarily relate to values and institutions which have a continuous history, though a tendentious plea to that effect is always advanced. So far as the characterisation is not fulfilled, it must relate either to an imaginary, romanticised past or to traditions which have been eroded beyond recognition, and in any case is strongly ideological (i.e. it not only legitimates the existing order by appealing to certain, presumed latent values in society, such as nationalism, but requires conforming action in so far as its propositions, especially those of more hierarchical, anti-individualistic, implication, are at the present time merely 'ideal'). But overtly, 'M.I.B.', standing for the Malay formulation *konsep Melayu Islam Beraja*, seeks to consolidate (after first asserting the ready existence of) a single national identity, born of convergence on a dominant Malay culture, and long binding a loyal citizenry to an absolute monarch of the same race, with the blessing and divine sanction of Islam. Originally, the professed purpose of the ideology, with its vision of virtually unchanging perfection across time, was no more than to draw popular attention to the salient features of the socio-political system and its benefits (as described in the model), so as to evoke the modicum of awareness and conscious conformity needed for the system to maintain itself (the essentially 'natural order of things') against competing ideas. The foundations of M.I.B. were laid by Director of Information Ustaz Badaruddin (a cleric), in the year before independence, when the Seri Begawan Sultan (the abdicated Sultan Omar Ali Saifuddin) was still influential in the affairs of State and reputedly very accessible to the former.[26]

Ustaz Badaruddin was more careful than his imitators have been to say that the doctrine described the central governing, and sociologically dominant, features of Brunei society - in other words, the Brunei-Malay part - without implying that the other ethnic groups had ever or have already assimilated to this culture, or must be considered deviant and disloyal if they do not.[27] The non-Malays were invited, rather, to acknowledge the leading role of Malay culture, to honour Malay institutions of government including the absolute monarchy, and to respect Islam as the religion of State. Non-Muslim indigenes may not even have been mistaken in believing that 'Malay' culture was intended to be understood in a sense as comprehensive and eclectic as the political definition of the term in the 1961 Nationality Enactment, i.e. to include all seven indigenous ethnic groups. A difference can be detected, if not a strong one, between this inclusive/permissive position and the semi-fascist inclusive/unpermissive imputation that non-Malay (i.e. non-Muslim) indigenous groups lack enough authentic or valu-able culture to be considered anything better than 'sub-groups' of the dominant Malay population. In the terms of this emphasis, the latter alone are the authentic heirs to the country and entitled to demand that non-Muslim practices which offend them are kept out of sight, or, at the extreme, that the 'pagans' all convert to Islam, as a condition of tolerance.[28]

19

It may not be beside the point to remark that for the authors of the 1961 Nationality Enactment, assimilation to Malay culture was definitely a long-term aim of political incorporation, in the interests of greater Malay strength vis-à-vis the 'Chinese menace' or even to forestall the rise of mini-nationalisms among the various ethnic groups. At all events, contrary to the claims of ideology, the culture and religion of Bruneians are still far from uniform. Only the Brunei Malay dialect has been generally adopted by all as a lingua franca. The 'shortcomings' in the situation indicate the need to cajole the non-Malay population in the prescribed direction, through ideological suasion, liberally funded internal missionary activity and social pressure.[29]

At the same time, no little official energy is invested in exhorting the Malays themselves to know and maintain their unique culture - as if they were either ignorant, or had become neglectful, of it, despite its reputed distinction (a society in the grip of change, it may seem, rather than static in the way the model pretends!). A national politeness campaign in May 1990 stands to suggest that social deference is the Malay virtue whose decline among youth is most keenly deplored. It is no doubt ironic that the social modernisation which promotes assimilatory trends among non-Muslims almost independently of direct governmental action has the capacity to weaken the attachment of would-be carriers of the dominant culture to their own core values and identity. Official anxiety on this score may account for the discovery by government-sponsored intellectuals, aggressively advertised at Malay world cultural conferences, that the uniqueness of Brunei-Malay culture, including political culture, consists not in parochial peculiarity but in the survival of the once standard, pristine Malay forms which other countries of the region have lost. But it must count as a further irony that at a time when 'national cultural identity' is conventionally projected abroad by way of the visual and performing arts, the Brunei Malays' meagre objective residue has been further reduced by clerical demands for 'compatibility with Islam'.[30] On the other hand, performing arts of Islamic, Middle Eastern provenance with a fairly short history in Brunei are now misleadingly exalted as 'traditional'.[31] At the same time, even Brunei's famous golden cats - the heraldic supporters of the sultan's arms, recalling an ancient relationship with Majapahit - have been liquidated on religious grounds. And the sultan has turned Islamic principles to personal advantage, against Malay custom, by giving practically equal status to his second wife, whose humble origins would have ensured for her the status of concubine only two generations ago.

20

Meanwhile, as a further, and quite extraordinary, paradox (yet surely not without political purpose), the development of the Malay language as a medium of literary expression and analytical thought is being thwarted by the new 'bilingual education policy' which, since 1984, has given priority to English as the medium of instruction throughout the education system. Simultaneously the most promising students are forced into the science stream. The relevant conclusion is not necessarily that the regime was aiming to create a more Westernised generation. Possibly more to the point, a developing cultural vacuum could have promised an opportunity for a stronger Islamic and non-nationalist orientation of Malay identity, in the sense that fluency of expression in Malay would tend to become the monopoly of a small group educated in the religious schools. (In fact the majority of non-middle-class youth receive virtually no education at all, because the medium of instruction cannot be understood; but parents are reassured in the short term as Malay medium students under the former, split system, faced inequality of opportunity in government employment, and there is now the illusion of equality.) The fact that in this case language engineering belies the populist side of ideology simply strengthens the inference that ideology is an instrument of legitimation first and foremost, upholding an interest for whom the literal pursuit, in all respects, of the society described and prescribed by that instrument might be dysfunctional. At any rate, whatever the long-term and hidden goals of education policy in 1984, such policy has laid a felicitous foundation for success in the explicit drive for Islamisation which the reader will meet in Section X, where ideology (as revised) becomes a much more creative variable - if only because of its preceding, adaptive, response to a challenge from the environment itself. Even without challenge of that kind, the regime was conscious of a need to dilute the nationalist dimension of Malay identity (as will be argued in Section VII), and it is clear that a more Islamically-biased model, if it can be realised in practice, will promise a greater degree of stabilisation, though also less development.

Emphatically, Islam did not lack a certain primacy in overt State policy, even at the time of independence, with latent implications for the future definition of Malay identity in Brunei. It is notable that the primary purpose of internal missionary activity has been to raise the levels of commitment and conformity among the Muslims themselves (once more, youths are the primary target).[32] In this light, again, the 'truth' of M.I.B. seems to represent an ideal to be striven for rather than a clearly existent reality - but more especially, here, because the (one-sided) thrust of policy, rather than the (balanced) ideological model, is at odds with present social reality. At the same time, Muslims under pressure may at least take satisfaction from their clear statistical dominance in relation to other indigenous groups. However, the function for the Malays of the 'I' in M.I.B. could never be as a merely confirmatory and reassuring echo of the 'M' (though Malay culture is, by social definition, in Brunei as in the Malay Peninsula, a Muslim culture). Nor would the 'I' act simply to reassure Muslims in terms of itself (though no doubt the Malays could never accept any derogation from the position of Islam as the official religion). Above all, 'I' commands *political* obedience, and acts as a special, legitimating prop to 'B' (the monarchy), which protects and fosters it reciprocally.

Whether religion was the primary basis of political loyalty in the past is highly questionable; still, in conservative forms it complements the transmitted deference of Malay society, and has a clear potential to foster bonds of solidarity. Legitimation through religion might also seem to recommend itself as a counterbalance to real, or apparent, secular and cosmopolitan elements in the royal lifestyle - though what is highlighted, in practice, is the looming menace of secularism in the West. The latest twist in public instruction is to divert attention from secularism in Malay society as a whole by attacking the Christian, Orientalist and Zionist 'enemies' of Brunei society and State.[33]

Turning now to the 'B' as such: one may observe that absolute monarchy as an institution of Brunei life has been - or has certainly become - considerably more pervasive and penetrating than either Islam or Malay culture. This seems a remarkable phenomenon, when one reflects that the Brunei sultanate was about to be undermined by revolts and flight of population as late as 1905, when the British intervened to save it, and faced an even more deadly rebellion as recently as 1962. However, even if the 1962 rebellion was not solely anti-British in its intent, the standing of the monarchy had been much improved by British action to stamp out aristocratic rapine and tribal marauding early in the century. The generalisation about the 'pervasive penetration' by absolute monarchy today may be subject to a subtle reservation about the sultan's dependence on the cooperation of powerful bureaucrats and the support of his own family, but the sultan has succeeded in creating a new, basic community or coalition of interest between himself and the top bureaucratic echelons by paying them, since 1984, far above international rates for equivalent ability and work. And obedience to the State is an undeniable facet of Brunei behaviour in society as a whole, above the level of petty regulations. However, although a personalised form of obedience to the sultan is internalised as a norm of the middle-aged and older generation of all ethnic groups, the incursions of universalistic values among younger, educated Bruneians today must be expected to make obedience more conditional on factors such as a high and increasing level of welfare, education opportunities and promotion. At least the government seems to assume such a prospect, seeing the decline of deference generally within Brunei's would-be 'enduring natural order'. Hence the imperative not only to exalt absolute monarchy as an ineluctable fact of present existence but, alongside its high religious merit, to advance a claim of structural continuity - a feature calculated to enhance not only legitimacy but probably the aura of unshakability too. In case a vista of unbroken tradition should not be sufficient justification either, in the eyes of a modern generation, adaptive efforts have been undertaken lately to describe the functions of the monarch and his operative relationship with the people in specific and attractive terms, though also with historical back-up. But we propose to examine claims regarding the sultan's functions in society, including his religious attributes, in later sections. For the moment, attention is devoted to the thesis of continuity - the lack of interruption in the tradition.

VI. *The Ideological Construction of the Residency Period*

This thesis is linked, of course, to the proposition that Bruneians have preserved moral autarchy in face of the tests of the twentieth century. Moral autarchy and continuity (both primarily ideological tenets) are even invoked to justify the perpetuation of traditional or neo-traditional political structure far into the future - in principle forever[34] - while the perception that, specifically, the British Residency (1906-1959) had little impact explains the frequent use of the term 'full independence' in official communication. And if Brunei never lost its independence properly speaking, needing only to repossess the peripheral areas of foreign policy and external defence, the purported continuity of political structure, over and above the vaunted absence of mass Asian immigration, since the 19th century, had left Brunei with nothing to struggle for, and nothing to struggle against (unlike the sultanate's neighbours in their time), as 1984 approached. Dramatic political changes were superfluous, it was argued, as well as potentially destructive; there was no need to equate independence with a change of regime or political system.[35] Appropriately, the independence celebrations were kept subdued, with a strong religious connotation, and National Day was instituted on 23 February, avoiding any commemoration of a 'hand-over of powers' as such.[36]

There are in fact two types of perspective on the British Residency: those which acknowledge it at least as an interlude; and another which overlooks it, more or less, in focusing on earlier and later periods of the British connection. A perspective of the first type featured dominantly in the arguments of the director of information during 1983. The Residency existed, and exercised substantial delegated power, in the first half of the 20th century - powers whose recovery by Bruneians would of course constitute an assertion of independence. But the occasion of such assertion was not to be 1984, for it had effectively taken place in 1959 when the British Resident exchanged his title for that of 'Her Majesty's High Commissioner'.[37] Subject to the provisos that the sultanate of 1959 was vastly more powerful than that of 1900, and that 1959 saw the rise of 'self-government' rather than 'independence' (Badaruddin himself forbore to use the actual term 'independence' in connection with the rise of the Constitution), the essence of the analysis is close to reality. Ustaz Badaruddin incurred not a little hostility in Bruneian circles at the time, both for deflating the significance of the 1984 transfer of residual powers (which nationalists would have liked to celebrate with more jubilation)[38;] and for pointing out obliquely that an absolute monarchy had been ensconced for fully twenty-five years and was not likely to relinquish its powers now (a fact which even some highly placed officials with political ambition had somehow over-looked).[39] Nevertheless the term 'full independence' is generally accepted, today, for what happened in 1984, and (Pehin) Ustaz Badaruddin was brought back as director of both information and broadcasting, as well as a permanent secretary in the prime minister's department, based in the palace, at the end of 1988.[40]

But an important variation on the theme of the Residency as 'interlude' maintains that British intervention was, from the start, far less purposeful or complete than in the sultanates of the Malay Peninsula. As far as the degree of Western economic penetration and educational development before 1959 are concerned, the generalisation is undoubtedly valid: apart from the oilfield, Brunei suffered (or perhaps benefited) from a regime of 'benign neglect'. (Had it been otherwise, the choice of a highly conservative monarchy to succeed provisionally to the powers of the Residency, and rule this relatively backward society in 1959, might have been even more difficult for British officials to countenance than it already was.) Yet to sustain the claim that Brunei was a more perfect example of merely indirect rule than even the five unfederated Malay States of Malaya had been - States which, despite a formal structure of indirect rule, did not doubt that they had been colonised, and celebrated independence with the rest of the Federation of Malaya in 1957 - it would be less than fitting for the Brunei State to illuminate strongly every aspect of the Residency Agreement of 1905. That agreement actually placed more power in the hands of the British Resident than occurred formally even in the four Federated Malay States.

The inconvenient reality is that by 1900 Brunei faced extinction through further sale of customary territorial rights to foreigners by the upper class. Revolts were playing into the hands of Charles Brooke (if not fomented by him). It was to pre-empt further erosion that the British not only established the Residency but armed it with powers to intervene in 'custom', leaving only the sphere of religion under the sultan's control.[41] By contrast, in the other Malay States custom as well as religion was reserved to the sultans, immune from the British Resident's or adviser's binding advice. (This is not to deny that British Residents of the peninsula sometimes interfered in custom and religion - as McArthur as first Brunei Resident would also do in religion - nor that centralisation substantially eroded the autonomy of the Federated Malay States. The issue is the written terms of the original Residency Agreement, to which Brunei officially attaches key significance.) In face of such a profound derogation from its sovereignty, official Brunei has allowed itself a little historiographical licence. Starting from 1967, the year of the abdication, when the historical section in the annual report for the first time included a retrospect on the achievements of Sultan Omar Ali Saifuddin and removed the usual reference to the approximately thirty concubines of his grandfather, Sultan Hashim, we learn that the 1905 agreement reserved both custom and religion to the authority of the latter[42] (albeit the full and correct text of the agreement is reproduced 16 pages later).[43] The 1967 statement of the case has been repeated in every history section in annual reports down to the present.[44] It also occurs in briefing papers distributed to foreign embassies in Brunei in 1989[45,] and Lord Chalfont has lent his name to it[46.]

Meanwhile, a Brunei educationist contributing a section to a stop-gap resource book for Brunei secondary school teachers has been subject to pressure to conform in this matter, but seems to have opted for a compromise whereby (not unlike the *Annual Report 1967*) the content of the agreement is quoted correctly but described in the diametrically opposite sense.[47] A foreign teacher who rushed to meet the urgent need for a secondary school textbook when an 'independence syllabus' was introduced has likewise decided to face two ways at once.[48] Much more ingenious, at first sight, is the approach adopted by the convenor of the state ideology course at Brunei's university, who in order to equate the experience of Brunei with other Malay States quotes an Anglo-Bruneian agreement which indeed accords the spheres of both religion and custom to the sultan; but it turns out, upon close examination, to be the Brunei Agreement of 1959.[49] Whether the writer in question was attempting consciously to strengthen a weak case may be questioned however in the light of two 'more mainstream' papers which assert that religion and custom were reserved to the sultan in 1905 - the latest of these two papers being an official handout on the Universiti Brunei Darussalam (UBD) state ideology course.[50] It is apparent that national historiography, like the writing or rewriting of constitutions, is a basic prerogative of the ruler and his government, and that statements bearing this imprimatur command wide respect and may be incorporated into local academic orthodoxy. Still, their acceptance is not yet enforced in a totalitarian way, except in schools. The text of the 1905 Supplementary Agreement (as it was known) is on display at the Constitutional Exhibition in the Brunei capital. Moreover, staff of the Brunei History Centre have been free to analyse the content and background of the agreement in an academic spirit.[51]

The inherent thesis of the majority view of 1905 is that British administration was rather too much in the mould of Indirect Rule, in effect, for its cessation at any time to be termed an act of 'independence'; and this points transitionally away from the conception of 'independence in 1959' towards the ultimate crowning vision of a Brunei which never experienced any outside intervention in its administration whatsoever. The preamble of the 1984 Proclamation of Independence (paradoxically so called) has elevated oblivion regarding the Residency period to the status of faith. Not only had Brunei 'never been a colony', but it was simply resuming, in accordance with the Treaty of 1979, the full international responsibility placed in British hands by the Protectorate Agreement of 1888. The only intermediate event mentioned is the Constitution of 1959, "in accordance with which the government of this State is ordered, constituting the highest law thereof."[52] This event (1959) can only be equated with any form of 'independence' if at least some form of prior derogation from internal administrative sovereignty is acknowledged. Since this is completely denied here, the term 'independence' really does become redundant. It is as inapplicable, logically, to 1959 as to 1984.[53] The 1959 Constitution itself is seen as the gift of the sultan, not the British, who were merely protectors. Concomitantly, as protection was their only role in this innovative Brunei doctrine, the sultan experiences no compunction in condemning them for withdrawing from that responsibility, in some of his statements directed towards audiences abroad.[54]

VII. *Legitimation from the Distant Past*

It may be almost a truism that authoritarian States whose subjects are exposed to democratic and universalistic values or egalitarian religion (or where the rulers are conquerors or migrant aliens), are more likely to seek legitimation through some kind of origin myth than popularly-based ones. Communist elites (as a new ruling class seeking an ideology of stabilisation) would invoke a myth of class struggle to obscure the dynamics of the party's seizure of power. Southeast Asian monarchies of the past created genealogies reaching back to a heavenly forefather. Certain Southeast Asian dominant party regimes of today have exaggerated the significance of nationalist struggle in their origins, by purporting to find it in local millenarian-type revolts of the 19th century.

For the contemporary Brunei sultanate there is room for some appeal to be made to the names of 19th-century territorial governors who resisted the encroachments of the British adventurer James Brooke (Sarawak's first 'white rajah'). But memories of 20th-century nationalism are entirely dysfunctional to the present political structure, for not only did the PRB rebellion of 1962 represent a struggle for democratisation as much as a stand against the British and Malaysia, but the nationalist movements in Malaya, Singapore, Indonesia and the Philippines likewise equated independence with democratisation and indeed achieved independence from their respective colonial masters on the very condition, or nominal condition, that the successor State would uphold democracy. Moreover, one of Brunei's neighbours adopted a threatening posture in favour of Brunei's democratic movement in the 1970s, as we have seen, causing regime survival to become equated, in some minds, with the issue of territorial integrity and survival. This engendered the almost pathological dependency syndrome of a client state resisting the pressure for independence exerted by the protecting power, and the sultan's later recriminations.[55] But the sultanate had already rejected the symbols of conventional nationalist struggle (primarily because of its dangerous connotations aforesaid) and begun to seek legitimacy in its own continuity. Since continuity from the 19th century has been linked to the denial that the British interlude was significant in reducing 'administrative sovereignty', the nationalist struggle may be viewed as superfluous anyway. Least of all may it be admitted that there was a threat, at the end of the 19th century, to continuity from earlier eras, and a collapse of political cohesion and loyalty, pointing to a potential extinction which only British intervention warded off. This would be tantamount to saying that modern Brunei was a 'creation of colonialism'.[56]

Now a political order which is thrown back on its more distant political structure as the foundation of its legitimacy may face a peculiar dilemma: that despite the relative conservatism of the present institutional arrangements, the State cannot afford to imitate traditional forms to the letter. How, for instance, could the Brunei sultanate, with its pretensions to be a 'member of the international community', dismantle the bureaucratic structure bequeathed by the British and other symbolic or performance-oriented appurtenances of a modern state? How, for that matter, could it dispense with the bureaucratic capacity to distribute material welfare - an 'output' far more vital to stability than any political legitimation by appeal to a tradition? And ironically, even historic expressions of royal power (not uniquely on the eve of British intervention) often fell short of pretension, yielding scant edification to model-seekers. The solution which has been taking shape - in the felicitous absence of any very precise knowledge about Brunei's more remote past - is to theorise ideologically about today's political order (the 'Malay, Islamic monarchy'), then project this essence backwards in time onto the principal historic structures, which, being thereby infused, may reflect the same light forward once more and suffuse the present order (however diffusely) with an aura of 'historic splendour'. For instance - an outstanding example - precedents for patriotism and Brunei-Malay-Muslim national identity are discovered in a fictional guerilla war to drive out the Spanish in 1579,[57] while there are signs, conversely, of attempts to erase the memory of a more authentic guerilla army, the *Tentera Nasional Kalimantan Utara* (National Army of North Kalimantan) of 1962.[58] With regard to Islam and the monarchy, the concern has been to enhance both the sanctity and glory of the early sultanate in popular perception, by intensive reference to a descendant of the Prophet.[59] Also, not entirely incidentally, an earlier origin is claimed for the Muslim Kingdom of Brunei than for Malacca itself.

The question of the age of the sultanate - i.e. the dating of the conversion of the monarchy - has become a policy question for the Brunei State and it may not be far-fetched to see a connection between an associated controversy and the hastened departure of a leading historian of Southeast Asia from

Brunei's shores. The detail of the controversy is of scant interest for the non-specialist, but it is important to realise at least the determination and ingenuity that have gone into making a case for Brunei's historical precedence among sultanates east of Sumatra. Robert Nicholl's latest and most versatile refutation of 1363, in favour of 1515, only tackles the problematic use of Ming Dynasty sources on the Brunei side.[60] What is perhaps more notable is the endeavour of the *de facto* state historian, a protégé of the late Sultan Omar Ali Saifuddin, to show that the first Brunei sultan received his title, regalia and religion (and a Muslim queen), not merely from the Malacca line before it was expelled by the Portuguese to Johore,[61] but before it had established itself even in Malacca, i.e. during its sojourn in Singapore on the way from Sumatra: for according to a sensational version of the Brunei Chronicle brought to light in 1971, the first sultan of Brunei was converted and crowned by the legendary king of Singapore, Sri Tri Buana.[62] This is the very first appearance of Sri Tri Buana in a Brunei text. But more astounding still, even if the sojourn in Singapore were accepted to have spanned a number of reigns, the Malacca Chronicle itself does not acknowledge the conversion of the Malacca Dynasty until seven generations after its founder.[63] One will probably search in vain for any other case of the legendary founder of a Malay dynasty, previously regarded as a Hindu, being discovered to have been a Muslim, least of all by a chronicler of another dynasty. But the 'discovery' does felicitously point to an 'electoral succession' bestowed by the Malacca line, yet 'before Malacca' - an excellent pedigree without the disadvantage of posteriority![64]

In general, the dynamics of the Bruneian dialectic which the ideology infers may be clarified by reference to the non-analogy of Marxism (here we are referring to Marxism as an ideology in its own right, with its own historical preconceptions, rather than the tool of sociological analysis which so brilliantly illuminates others' ideas). Where Marxism sees history as a process of profound change in which successive periods prepare the way for the future but cannot prefigure it, the emergent Brunei ideology appears to see history as a series of pre-manifestations of its own central, defining propositions. If there is an implicit progression, it may be in the Hegelian mould, towards the ever more perfect expression of an underlying idea. Although this has yet to be spelled out, appeals to Brunei historians to fill the gaps in national history are certainly not to be taken in the sense of desiring a critical evaluation of the hypothesis of continuity. Continuity of power and its close ally, ancient pedigree - along with several other propositions - are ideological tenets, more akin to fruits of revelation than to findings of research.[65]

30

Of course, it is hardly necessary to recall that the generation of ideology as such, in defence of an established power position, is completely predictable under Marxian sociological assumptions.[66] Nor is it surprising to find that the ultimate beneficiaries of political transformation during this century have adopted an ideology which envisages future change as little as it admits genuine historical process in the past, treating the present as a minor Age of Perfection, within Brunei's borders at least.[67]

VIII. A Theory of Social Contract

But the sultanate is realistic at the same time: borders are highly 'penetrable'. More worrying than any growth of universalistic values through socio-economic transformation is the phenomenon of direct democratic influences emanating from neighbouring countries and the world media, and a certain egalitarian current in Islamic fundamentalism. Thus, to forestall a 'decline of deference', it has been thought necessary to soften the harsh outline of absolute monarchy in the ideological model by theorising about a 'social contract'. This principle is clearly in conflict with divine right, but on the Brunei scene almost has the benefit of anticipating it, for the latter has also received little prominence till now. (The unequal power and wealth of monarchs are normally seen as a manifestation of Malay customary practice, not of Islam, though Islam has been ever ready with rationalisation.) As defined by the director of information, the 'social contract' comprises an on-going extra-constitutional compact whereby the people agree to surrender their political rights and the monarch reciprocally eschews tyranny.[68] In other words, the Brunei ideology itself was being adjusted here in the interests of its own legitimacy, as if the mere reiteration of absolute monarchy as a fact of existence now and in the past cannot be trusted to convert it into an accepted norm.

Since democratic influences and the notion of a 'contract' have the potential to make citizens regard many manifestations of executive, let alone royal, power as 'tyrannical' and *ergo* opposable, it seems surprising at first sight that 'tyranny' has not been defined, either by the director of information or any of the university lecturers involved in ideological propagation. Their silence may be taken to imply that tyranny, even by the broadest definition, is inconceivable. Or is it simply feared that attempts to define a limiting case may stimulate the public to excogitate sundry definitions of tyranny (and thereby the possibility of its existence) where none existed before? There is, as it happens, a sentimental strand in peninsular Malay folktales and poetry which suggests that obedience is conditional on the 'justice of government'. For the time being, this tradition may serve to foster an acquiescent assumption among Bruneians that their ruler can be relied upon to be just if the people are obedient, whereas public discussion of the nature of 'justice' and 'tyranny' might well work to expose the illogicality of this comfortable belief. Certainly, evidence of the compact as an institution of contemporary Brunei is more difficult to pin down than any of the basic elements in 'M.I.B.' - not least because monarchical power in historically unprecedented concentration *is* its objectively most verifiable element!

It is conceivably in anticipation of these difficulties that history is mobilised once again, where it is claimed that the social contract was adopted by the monarchy along with Islam, in the 14th century. Here the apparent purpose is not just to cast an aura of ancient dignity on a contemporary phenomenon, but to lend credibility to a doubtful construct by locating its origin 'deep in the mists of time', where experts alone may penetrate. Yet if experts do penetrate, they will only encounter further problems. The earliest reference to a social contract that has yet come to light, notwithstanding the best efforts of the apologists, is contained in a text of their own forerunner, a servant of the previous monarch.[69] Sultan Omar Ali Saifuddin was himself a poet and historical romantic of no mean proportions, it may be added. Herein may lie a clue to the mysteriously late appearance of this, the first documentary expression of the doctrine - though not too late to have anticipated the promulgation of the Brunei Constitution by one year and to act, perhaps, as its informal preamble of intent: a declaration of absolute prerogative, in fact, combined with voluntary restraints.[70] No earlier statement of the doctrine came to the attention of the leading historian of Brunei social structure, still unrivalled - an American writing in the late 1960s.[71] It does reappear fleetingly in a strange 17th century law code brought to light and published in 1973,[72] three years too late to escape all suspicion of having the purpose of riposte to the American, who had had the temerity to write of the unreliability of local accounts of the historic functions and powers of political offices.[73] The more authentic late-17th-century Brunei Chronicle gives scant indication of the duties of a sultan towards the people, except the building of a State mosque: and here the emphasis is all on the merit accruing to the sultan and the high officials principally involved, with rules for seating the population at prayer strictly according to social rank.[74]

Faced with such paucity of local evidence for the historic 'social contract', ideologues of sundry nationality at the Brunei university have been seeking analogues in early Malacca, with a determination surely born of desperation. One may infer desperation since the classic contract between the legendary *non*-Muslim founder of the Malacca dynasty-to-be, Sri Tri Buana, and his chief minister, Demang Lebar Daun, even if it could be presumed to have been known and copied by the early Muslim rulers of Brunei in the same way as Muslim religion, does not allow revolt on the grounds of tyranny any more than Islam does. The only *casus foederis* recognised are cases, somewhat hypothetically and intangibly, of rulers putting their subjects to 'shame' - a peculiarly aristocratic taboo, not inspired by anything at all proximate to a concept of popular rights, however conditional.[75]

The reinterpretation of the Malaccan covenant by an Indonesian linguistic authority is indeed not the least astonishing of early developments on the UBD ideology course.[76] In fact, Professor Teuku follows a Dutch anthropologist, de Jong, in describing the covenant as a 'social contract', but de Jong, as quoted, appears to regard it as comparable with the Magna Carta - whose feudal rather than democratic inspiration is widely understood. Indeed the Malay covenant is arguably less progressive than Magna Carta, in its exclusion of tyranny as a justification even of aristocratic revolt. But what makes the whole ideology of the just, Muslim ruler substantially irrelevant to the people of Brunei in early times is the fact that in early times - and even quite recent ones - most of the subjects of the sultans outside a few coastal enclaves were not Muslim.[77]

IX. The 'Contract' in Action: 'A Nationalist Sultan'?

In the course of the preceding section we found that the social contract idea seems to go back no further than the previous reign - to be precise, to the period of the drafting of the Constitution - and that even then it was not a case of monarchy becoming subject to anything more than voluntary restraints, purely self-imposed and conditional upon the obedience of the population. In the next section the unambivalent vitiation of contractual thinking through religious orthodoxy will receive our attention. This may be considered more prudent, and consistent with the Seri Begawan's vision, as well as avoiding the invocation of spurious precedents for a social contract from the distant Malay past. If the distant past is to be invoked, it should at least be in a way that is functional to political priorities, such as conjuring an ancient popular monarchism![78] But admittedly the distant past is generally 'safer' as a source of any purported precedent, being beyond the reach of memory if not of research, and less prone to refutation.

Brunei is a country which never ceases to surprise. As a political adviser to the Brunei monarchy - if vouchsafed such a desirable, highly remunerated position - one might hesitate to recommend any intensive focus on the reign of the late sultan. Indeed this was generally the instinct of the regime itself up to 1989, because of the 'unfortunate' turn taken by Brunei nationalism. Yet the urge to overlay novelty with a veneer of historical continuity would appear to have taken on the force of an addiction. Since about the middle of 1989 an interest began to become manifest in professional historical circles in Brunei, concerning the role of the late sultan, Omar Ali Saifuddin III: not as the ruler who had no need of nationalism because his country was never colonised, but as the patriot who himself fostered the nationalist spirit and led his people towards true independence in the face of contrary British interest and intention (the North Borneo Federation and Malaysia proposals), not to speak of an attempt by the PRB to 'steal his nationalist clothes' and usurp his position in a treacherous revolt. It is much to the benefit of the present presentation that a quotable text has become available which exposes the basic propositions of this interesting strand of historical revisionism.[79] No doubt the appearance of the article in question is not a unique or chance event but more like the pointing 'straw in a wind' that is likely to prove prevailing, if one may judge from the growing cult of the Seri Begawan evidenced by the prayers for his soul at every meeting of government departments, the frequent asperges of his tomb by relays of government servants, the not much less frequent claims by the sultan that he is guided by his late father's inspiration, talk of plans for a special Seri Begawan Museum, and, in June 1991, the dispatch of a team of writers drawn from UBD and the History Centre to scour the British Public Records Office for edifying reference on the late ruler's nationalist ideals.

In terms of ideological historiography, four pages of the article contain all the more instructive passages.[80] Limitations of space have precluded the publication of a translation as an appendix to the present study; but this is not to play down its importance. The analytical responses which the extract evokes relate, firstly, to the startling degree of inconsistency between the historiographical emanations of diverse government agencies. In this case it is the History Centre staking out new ground in opposition to the drafters of the independence declaration. But it is not the first time that History Centre staff have done this with reference to colonialism in Brunei,[81] and the effort in the latest instance is complementary with the director of the History Centre's concern to establish in the minds of Bruneians a faith in their capacity for self-government (as at the launch of his book in 1991), despite an implied history of tutelage. Secondly, however, one could take the latest development as a sign of the regime's capacity not just for ideological innovation but for 'second generation' ideological renewal or revision in response to evolving environmental challenge, or perception thereof, in reallocating responsibility for interpreting national history. And what, thirdly, may that perceived challenge comprise? Arguably, a suspected failure of previous historical legitimation to show any great impact: precisely because the chosen reference points in the past were so remote and intangible.

The advantage of developing popular consciousness of continuity from the recent past is that memories of the elderly Seri Begawan are still fresh, while for his life as a whole there is ample documentation, including photo and film which will be available to be shown long after memories have faded. On the other hand (and fourthly), the crucial 1950s are sufficiently remote to rising generations for the government's new interpretation not to clash with any contrary recollections or preconceived ideas of most 'consumers'. In any society with a strong sense of its past beyond propagated stereotypes, the new strategy would be fraught with risk, but in Brunei society generally the said condition and the accompanying danger may be absent, in the government's view. (The fact that a book full of highly 'explosive' material on the autocratic and thoroughly un-independence-minded late sultan has entered Brunei in considerable quantities without ever exciting the interest of the Special Branch could be an indication of an - undoubtedly justified - complacency in government circles.)[82]

It follows, fifthly, that the 1950s offer an ideal field for the development of 'background' for the present-day official view of the monarchy's role as the guardian of national sovereignty and the people's welfare purely on terms decided by the monarchy itself. This view is of course compatible with, in fact derived from, the Seri Begawan's one-sided version of a 'social contract'. There is genuine continuity of outlook here. The 'legacy of history' can scarcely be disputed in this respect. Nevertheless, the few Bruneians who ever summon the interest and find the time to read up the period from non-Brunei writers will meet disturbing divergences between the latter and the local 'authorities' with regard to the late sultan's 'nationalist leadership': the actual, pragmatic benefit that his type of social contract yielded to the people. It may take a leap of faith to accept that autocratic absolutism was consistent with, indeed expressed, the popular will, where at a time of burgeoning political communications and colonial pressure for constitutionalism the ruler commanded no body of followers or clients except his own bureaucracy and district administration; the mass party which in general principle shared the desire of the protecting power to move towards independence via constitutional reform, and was at odds with the ruler because the latter apparently did not, won all the seats in the assembly at the first general elections; and the same party took its desperate opposition to the Malaysia plan to the point of rebellion, seeing so many signs that the ruler was about to be inveigled by the British into merger and 'false independence', having already given a prominent role to seconded Malayan civil servants in his bureaucracy.

The fact that there was a gulf of political ideals and aims between the politically organised population and the sultan, and that this, rather than a straightforward anti-colonial uprising, was what the PRB's desperate act was essentially about, is felicitously inferred by the Seri Begawan's budding biographer, where he refers to the rebellion as *penderhakaan*.[83] This concept of 'treachery to a king', heavy with historical resonance, evokes the horror and fear of divine retribution that Europeans might once have felt in face of regicide and incest, both taboos being broken in combination. It is more heinous than 'treason of State'. It breaks a personal bond with the ruler. *Derhaka* was what the descendants of Demang Lebar Daun were bound by their legendary contract *not* to be towards the seed of Sri Tri Buana. *Derhaka* was what the sultans of late 19th century and early 20th century Malaya were sometimes obliged by a British Resident or adviser to accuse their subjects of being, when the latter rose against the British.[84] Conceivably there was some British influence in play when the sultan used the term on 19 December 1962.[85] But the author who has used the term in this recent, pioneering essay on that sultan is not Sir Dennis White, the British high commissioner of the time, but a Bruneian whose career as an historian only began after Brunei's independence. His judgement on the nature of the rebellion deserves to be taken seriously, the more so as he is not reluctant, in general, to choose the 'optimum' or more complimentary possible interpretations of the late sultan's motives and actions: witness Muhammad Hadi's use of a royal speech of 1963[86] to illustrate the sultan's 'independence struggle', when in fact His Highness was advertising and justifying a trip to Kuala Lumpur to proceed into the final stage of discussions for political merger with the mainland. True, if one proposed that the PRB were conducting an anti-British campaign, it would detract from the sultan's own nationalist credentials, and that is clearly ruled out for this biographer; but by stating so firmly that the rebels were guilty of *penderhakaan*, the biographer shows how distant even a benign absolutist monarch may become from the real sentiments of his people and how easily forfeit their loyalty.

It is not the present writer's wish to discredit this Brunei historian with regard to his interpretation of royal self-perception, inasmuch as the late sultan was probably quite sincerely convinced that dynastic interest was compatible, nay, identical with, popular interest. It is also otiose to discuss what the 'real interest' of the people comprised, least of all who was 'right' and who was 'wrong', for these are purely matters of opinion or personal philosophy. The only questions at issue, historically, are whether an alternative view of popular interest was being advocated with equal conviction by spokesmen appointed in some sense by the people themselves (thus expressing a more authentic 'popular will'); and whether 'the third party' - the British government - had a view of popular interest which (even if reinforced by some considerations of British interest, as would be natural, with emphasis now on Malaysian Federation instead of the Borneo Federation idea which had previously brought the British and PRB together) was still fundamentally closer to that of the PRB than to that of the sultan. If both these questions were to be answered affirmatively, it would transpire that the Seri Begawan's conception of a 'social contract', although certainly *of* the modern era (being his own romantic blueprint for dynastic viability in a new age) was yet strangely out of touch with it. It would also follow that where rival views of popular interest in any respect were strongly opposed to each other, the royal view could only prevail with the help of force in the short term, or, in the long term, if at all, with the help of intensive indoctrination in order to bring the rival views into harmony. It may be suggested that the recent development in historical revisionism, focusing on the reign of the late sultan, is indeed part of an ongoing strategy for the 'coordination' of rival Bruneian visions.

Specifically, although the concept of a social contract is not mentioned in Muhammad Hadi's study, it does surely constitute his essential, if hidden, concern. He is committed to showing that all the Seri Begawan's judgements were for the best in terms of his people's welfare. History is being mobilised to show that an 'enlightened ruler' need not be questioned, least of all opposed; that a 'contract' can be one-sided but still meaningful and productive as a pillar of commonwealth. Total acceptance of this basic, general proposition by all Bruneians is not the least condition for enduring political stability, precisely because the asymmetry of the 'contractual relationship' is so divergent from the dynamics of contracts in other modern spheres. Without total acceptance or 'suspension of disbelief', the claims of the monarchy could even in themselves generate opposition and instability. It is only in this light that we can fully understand the importance of didactic historical demonstration - the discovery of a positive 'test case'.

But the fact that the official historiographer has to beg the gigantic question whether the legacy of the 1950s (the present political structure, which can indeed be dated to that period) is indeed 'for the best' for all Bruneians, is not without inconvenience. Perhaps this is why he puts more emphasis on gaining independence. Certainly if the Seri Begawan had prepared the way for true independence (or people can be persuaded that he did), this would provide the biographer with an ideal means of showing that royal absolutism is in the people's interest: either directly, because of what it has yielded, or indirectly by casting its proven aura of virtue from the 1950s upon the present sultan. Yet it is the devastating irony of the chosen example that the Seri Begawan's tactics for 'independence' were those on which most politically alert people disagreed with him most of all; in fact their disagreement went to the point of rejecting his good faith as a raja 'of the people' altogether.

At any rate - to summarise - the task the official writer of modern Brunei history faces cannot sensibly be that of legitimating a structure by appeal to its 'longevity'. That would be awkward, for though the 1950s may be 'semi-remote' for the younger generation, to some extent a focus on that decade takes the risk of highlighting contemporary change, not continuity. Rather, therefore, he must argue its specific utilitarian value. But since the value of the structure may not be manifest to all Brunei subjects, resort must be had to the independence issue in turn. However, that issue is also extremely problematic and potentially leads back to the notion that what was really at stake for the sultan was the political structure and what it offered his family, and that this structure, not independence, is the more significant legacy of that period. It redounds to the biographer's credit that he does not ultimately hide (despite parallel references to a 'struggle' culminating in 1984) that the critical struggle was the one by which royal control of the State apparatus was wrested in 1959. In this respect, Muhammad Hadi is in accord with Pehin Badaruddin. *This* was the Seri Begawan's 'independence'. From such a perspective, the other, in 1984, was irrelevant if not dangerous - except (the only important lacuna in Muhammad Hadi's account) that 1959 realised its fullest structural significance retrospectively, in 1984 itself, after the remaining legislative provisions of the Constitution were abolished (a desperate throw which yet confirms how dangerous full independence was felt to be, and explains why the Seri Begawan so long resisted it). What is very new, at odds with Badaruddin, is the position that Brunei did, after all, need some form of nationalism.

In case Brunei citizens in any numbers should come to perceive 1959 as the beginning of a new era - and perceive it in a spirit that both discounts the credibility of the Seri Begawan's struggle for independence at a later date and questions the value, for the people, of the structure founded in 1959 - it would be possible to shift back to the thesis that the monarchy in 1959 was neither creating nor restoring anything, but fulfilling underlying patterns which had never been subject to any process of significant historical change. The first royal speech quoted by Muhammad Hadi, which denies that Brunei was colonised, is compatible with this approach. In this way the somewhat uncertain legitimacy from the recent past would be reinforced by the more distant perspective, embracing earlier patriarchs back to Alak Betatar.

X. *The Orthodox Affirmation*

Attempts to attribute genuine social contract theory to Islam are fraught with even more difficulty than seeking it in Brunei Malay tradition or the annals of pre-Muslim Malacca. (Does the attempt have to be made because the argument from Malay custom is itself not convincing?) We have observed that the Brunei public is not yet inclined to be critical of politically authoritative ideas, and it is predictable that few Muslim laymen will notice the shift in religious doctrine. However, the numerous religious officials with degrees from Al-Azhar University in Cairo are in a position to notice, and perhaps to question. Muslim doctrine is a corpus of belief that is essentially fixed by virtue of its revelatory nature. Reinterpretation is not allowed. At most, a mufti (the chief religious scholar in any state) may apply received doctrine to newly arising circumstances. In any case, in the matter of absolute monarchy the mufti of Brunei has shown no inclination to budge from the orthodox position that revolt is impermissible even against a tyrannical ruler. Only commands in conflict with Islam may be disobeyed.[87]

What the 'progressive' Brunei scholars are doing, in fact, when pressed for clarification, is to assert that the first sultan will have adopted a social contract 'tacitly', upon conversion, because Islam enjoins a ruler to rule justly. As far as it goes, this command of Islam is correctly stated, but it is not equivalent to a theory of social contract, which is logically ruled out by the orthodox position that if the ruler chooses nonetheless to be a tyrant, he cannot be overthrown by his subjects: his punishment will be in the hereafter.[88] It is therefore tempting to remark that the director of information has 'gone out on a limb' on behalf of his monarch. But it would be fair to add that a more senior cleric, no less a personage than the minister of religious affairs, Pehin Ratna Diraja, has done exactly the same.[89]

In the end, it may be hierarchy - indeed the pinnacle of hierarchy, working with its most dedicated allies - that will settle the contradiction in the light of their own perceived interest. The social contract idea is an astute concession to the spirit of a democratic age but in the long run might encourage destabilising speculation about the precise obligations and limitations encompassing an Islamic monarch. Orthodox prerogative, by contrast, is placed beyond debate by its own innate absolutism and transcendental sanction. And the higher bureaucratic echelons, both secular and religious, share the monarch's interest in limiting popular reflection on power.

In this light, it was not astonishing to hear a forthright speech by a leading statesman (the minister of education) in December 1989, affirming that sovereignty is an attribute of God, delegated in trust to a caliph. It is wrong - or certainly not relevant to Brunei - to see sovereignty or its associated rights as an attribute of the people, he stated.[90] The minister of religious affairs, too, has shown a more conservative side, in a carefully weighed major speech on the divine trust vested in a Muslim ruler.[91] Neither statesman failed to infer that the present 'caliph' does rule with justice (the merit of a good sultan is worth that of 60 virtuous companions, said Pehin Ratna Diraja pointedly). It is even explicit that the caliph receives his divine mandate on condition of just rule.[92] But it is very clearly the court of heaven that will judge whether the mandate has been abused or forfeited, not a tribunal of mortals sitting to determine a breach of contract.[93]

Meanwhile, the fact that the UBD Department of Islamic Studies has taken over the indoctrination of government officials since January 1990, applying Islamic political theory wholesale and untempered to the legitimation of the Brunei ruler, is suggestive of the future trend. And if Islam counterposes a vast storehouse of ready-made, coherent doctrine to the as yet inarticulate, uncodified ragbag of M.I.B., the corpus in question has the further advantage of being exempt from any empirical challenge. Its metaphysical absolutes in general are nicely in tune with the not-to-be-questioned power of the leading institution to whose aid Islam is summoned - notwithstanding that modernist Muslim opinion agrees with radical fundamentalism in attributing the present incoherence of M.I.B. to a permanent incompatibility of Islamic principles with both ethnic nationalism and traditional Malay monarchy (not to speak of extreme inequalities of wealth), nor that real charisma in a ruler seems alien to Sunnism too. It is not, anyway, intellectual compatibility that counts, but the fact that M.I.B. now symbolises, more than anything else, an officially sponsored Islamic revival.

The new wave of 'revival' - more a case of Islamisation *de novo* in the Brunei Malay context (the resort to orthodoxy is deceptive) and demanding much more substantial changes in Malay lifestyle - is a response in the first instance to a situation which it simultaneously highlights (and which has been previously discussed): the ever-doubtful legitimacy of absolute monarchy in the present era, and the positive dangers of Brunei nationalism or nationalist nostalgia for the monarchy's survival. (Even the Malay cultural identity which may have been the originally intended focus of the 'M' in M.I.B. is now being rewritten to a Middle Eastern specification, with increasing pressure on women to 'cover up', short of total purdah.) It seems ironical that although the orthodox clerics were also reacting, in part, against the 'social contract' theory, they were mainly, like Pehin Badaruddin himself, coming to the rescue of the monarchy. But this makes sense when we observe and acknowledge that Islamisation is designed more immediately to correct the image of the regime in face of growing fundamentalist criticism of its 'secularism' between 1986-88. The result is a reordering of the relative emphases within the State ideology that is considerably more dramatic (and likely to be more lasting) than the tentative and somewhat deviant play on a 'social contract'.

Perhaps the most interesting aspects of this development, or connected with it, are that (a) while the Sunni establishment proceeds to promote royal absolutism under divine mandate, it sees even more the enhancement of its own power to dictate social behaviour and political norms under the sultan's reciprocal sanction;[94] (b) even in these new conditions of dynamic and symbiotic coalition, the handful of local activists of the Malaysian-based Al-Arqam movement whose activities first prompted, it seems, the new official emphasis on religion, have still not reconciled themselves with monarchy (in consequence, their movement and its dreaded, Shi'a-type theological tendencies have been subject to a banning edict since February 1991; but without doubt their influence will continue to alarm the sultan and make him seek to justify, balance, or simply conceal absolutism by further increments of Islamisation);[95] and (c) analytically speaking, it begins to emerge that the official ideology is not simply inaccurate in speaking of a particular 'static reality' (Arqam is a good case of both international 'penetration' and endogamous opposition) but is not perfectly tuned to its task of consolidating the ideal either. On the contrary, the new phase of Islamic indoctrination may have acted to illuminate, to the opposition, the seriousness of the monarchy's intent as to the perpetuation of absolutism; but it simultaneously provides, in Islam, a sanctified medium for the expression of opposition. (This will be true to the extent that the opposition is already prone to see any close association of Islam with monarchy as tending towards an abuse of religion in the interests of a temporal power.) In sum, a State structure which stood in need of strong popular support or at least acquiescence in order to confirm its ideological propositions as reality may face a decline of support in at least one quarter because those propositions underwent creative redefinition.[96]

43

In effect, we may analyse ideology as an independent variable in the Brunei sociological scenario, a bizarre and unintended factor activating social process. Admittedly, Arqam would have come to Brunei from Malaysia with or without the existence of State ideology. But it is not implausible that the shift in M.I.B. since 1986 has lately accelerated Arqam's growth, through provocation, just as Arqam's arrival initially pushed the regime into that redefinition of its ideology and a restructuring of its 'supporting coalition', for protection. Such interplay of ideas and social forces is likely to become more complex and dynamic if fundamentalist opposition spreads and is met with further, reactive tightening of orthodoxy-with-charismatic-overtones. Developments of this kind would alienate the non-Muslims and could make elements which favour economic development come to see incremental Islamisation, with its far-reaching attitudinal and behavioural connotations, as a block to their goals.

Further, and lastly, in this analytical vein, the point may be made (d) that when the descriptive dimension of an ideology undergoes any fairly sharp redefinition, its original account of social reality is potentially exposed as a self-serving sham. Now that the would-be timeless equilibrium of three forces is substituted by a model which gives the overwhelming emphasis to monarchy and religion as pillars of the Brunei order, it might occur (indeed has occurred) to an occasional thoughtful citizen that political interest is involved (namely the interests of monarchy and religious establishment) and that it was involved behind the old model as well.

One would hasten to add, however, that a few isolated analytical spirits, either fundamentalist or secularist, do not add up to a coalition of resistance, let alone a revolutionary force. It is the emergent ruling coalition that will keep the initiative and make the ideological running for some time to come in a society which is slow to conceptualise intellectual inconsistency, far less condemn it. Moreover, while some groups come closer to exclusion from the national community as the definition of 'Malay' becomes more Islamic, the sultan potentially steps forward as a more benevolent and inspired protector, or unifying nationalist surrogate, for the true Malays.[97]

XI. *The Dilemma of Development*

It has already been suggested that welfare is a far more important 'output' from the point of view of regime stability than any amount of ideology. It is therefore striking that the official ideology confines itself to an exercise in prescription-cum-description of a complex of sociological arrangements essentially static in nature, the last, not merely the latest stage (if at all 'stages' are acknowledged) in a process of historical self-fulfilment. In the context of pioneer 'M.I.B.' the younger generation were invited to 'consolidate' the legacy of history - thus the need for a degree of supportive input was admitted - but no greater degree of development or change in the basic relationships was envisaged. (In reality, no doubt, rather more social change than this would be necessary in order to 'return' society to its purported pristine state, so far as that has been eroded by modernisation; and more still to realise conservative Islamic forms never yet seen on Brunei soil; but these, by definition, are not unambiguously changes in a 'modernising' mould.) The essential paradox lies in the fact that at the same time some sort of self-sustaining economic development, and the maintenance of welfare levels and income in partial independence of oil revenues and government employment respectively, seem to be important goals of State policy. Calls to move with the age of high technology are heard every day. The government even boasts that Brunei is 'in process of unprecedentedly rapid development'.

A certain logic shines through the apparent illogicality. The spectre of limited oil reserves and generally depressed oil prices, while population growth accelerates, have come to dominate the horizons of the economic planners. But the economic goals and demonstration effect of government efficacy cannot be achieved without the mobilisation of the very population, particularly the younger potential workforce, which is simultaneously the *target* (as beneficiaries and consumers) of eye-catching infrastructural and public facility welfare projects and of welfare and income strategies. All this should pose a dilemma in relation to a static ideological model which maintains that the benefits of a truly Malay polity are conditional on full and unchanging adherence to the traditional Malay values of piety and political humility, and in relation to religious propagation which, among other things, would see women excluded from the work-force.[98]

In this connection one wonders whether the sultan was completely sincere in describing Brunei youth as 'future leaders' of his autocratic polity[99] or whether the director of broadcasting and president of the National Youth Council during 1987 was serious in describing youth as 'agents of development'.[100] And what of the proposition articulated by a government propaganda writer (echoing authoritative statements, of course) that youth will determine the shape of the nation in future and must therefore become an 'active' component of society?[101] Yet, however difficult to credit, such a theme has a history: it surfaced at least as early as 1968, when the young sultan described youth as a source of energy for change.[102] Nor had it shown signs of running out of steam 21 years later, since the speech from the throne on the sultan's 43rd birthday again spoke of the future leadership role of Brunei youth.[103]

A clue to the puzzle may perhaps be found in the role of Brunei's many registered youth organisations. A large proportion is in fact moribund. Recurrent government campaigns to infuse life into them do little more than highlight the phenomenon. It is a tempting presumption that the more enterprising kind of youth do not find a satisfying outlet for their energy in organisations which in practice only operate under tight government supervision. The urge to supervise is manifest, indeed, in many government statements which counterbalance or cancel out (sometimes within a single sentence) the 'future leaders' theme. In another speech in 1987 the 'national youth president' identified youth, significantly, as *supporters*, as well as 'agents', of development.[104] The sultan, in a speech to the Brunei Scout Movement in 1989, stressed the importance of discipline and respect for teachers and elders as Brunei youths prepared themselves for their future role as 'leaders'.[105] The minister of education, in a not uncharacteristic pronouncement, has emphasised the importance of fostering the Bruneian quality of deference in the schools.[106] This is in keeping with the idea that the education system comprises a set of government-bestowed facilities which it would be ungrateful not to make optimum use of.[107] The downright 'ungratitude' which the sultan sees in any opposition by former recipients of government training scholarships is tantamount to treason.[108] Meanwhile, the compulsory status of national ideology at the local university no doubt speaks for itself: at UBD, control of youth takes precedence over mental activation, and formalistic restraints upon the learning process prevail.[109]

It should be clear from the foregoing instances that talk of the 'future leadership role of Brunei youth', if not completely meaningless, has at least to be understood in terms of a peculiarly Bruneian meaning - one shaped by a political context remote from that of Malaysia, where the youth wings of political parties act as vocal critics and, on occasion, catalysts of government policy. Political participation in Brunei can only be on terms of submission to the will of the present ruling interest and its definition of developmental goals. The public declarations which can be taken seriously are those which laud the sultan's leading role in development,[110] and depict development as the government's gift to the people. Individuals are free to pursue personal economic goals within this framework but cannot seek to remould the framework as such, through political action, let alone to question its underlying political terms of reference.[111]

The 'Loyal Addresses' by district officers during the sultan's annual birthday progress around the four districts, which cannot be less than completely 'correct', are appropriately enshrined in a glossy publication entitled *The Will of the State*. One paragraph from the speech by the district officer of Temburong at the 1988 audience in his district will convey something of the flavour. Note that the district officer, though seeming to speak as the people's representative, is in fact the sultan's chief officer in the district.

> In response to the progress that we have enjoyed, the humble servants of Our Exalted Lord are united in their resolution and determination to strive together to implement all and any further plans and undertakings of the Government of My Exalted Lord, designed as they are purely for the welfare and prosperity of the citizens and residents of our beloved country. It is fitting that the citizens and residents of this District in particular, and of Brunei Darussalam in general, being filled with gratitude for the enjoyment of these several aspects of progress, should increase their efforts in sincerity and full social responsibility, take advantage of the various facilities which have been made available in order to make their own contribution to national development, and also build up their livelihood in ways consistent with the laws and regulations and according to individual capacity and ability.[112]

Now the Brunei government does not assume that criticism will be quelled simply by suppression. Economic development in itself is a tool of legitimation for the sultan, and only by meeting current popular expectation can the sultan justify his monopoly as 'leader of development' - purporting to exercise more than just a royal prerogative but almost an esoteric art, like the reputed ability of the last sultan, his father, to make rain. The government has to show 'performance' in the area of nationalist aspiration too, by restricting citizenship for Chinese, banning the Lion Dance from the streets of the capital, and setting a 75 percent promotion quota in Brunei Shell for indigenous staff. In this context, the proximity of Malaysia is functional to regime legitimacy and the denial of political participation, because the Malaysian plural society constitutes a negative model, from which the sultanate claims to have preserved, and to be preserving, its Malay subjects. This helps to project absolute monarchy as an asset of their race.[113]

The government even takes credit for the peaceableness and relative security of Bruneian society. Outsiders may attribute the present tranquillity of the 'Abode of Peace' more to a combination of ingrained docility in the population and its fear of security measures directed against itself if it lost the knack of 'compromise'.[114] But if such an attribution is correct, the government's confidence in its ability to keep control without any concessions to democracy must seem to be reasonably justified for the moment. At the same time, our argument that the 'agents of development' theme is to be understood more in the sense of 'servants of development', takes on enhanced conviction. Simultaneously it will be obvious that the sultanate's vision for youth is in contradiction with any authentic concept of social contract, in that, while the ruler is tacitly advised to aim for performance in the interests of regime legitimacy, he cannot be judged or challenged if in any way his performance falls short of expectation. Shortcomings in this respect are likely to be blamed on youth themselves, whose capacity for compromise and obedience had fallen below par. A recent elaboration to State ideology by the director of information and broadcasting, postulating that, in the absence of a political opposition, 'the people are part of the government',[115] is best taken to mean that since there is no overt difference of political opinion or interest in Brunei, the people's ineluctable destiny is to fulfil the government's will as if its own. It is certainly not fortuitous that the National Day pattern displays by requisitioned youth (the secondary school students of the capital, especially from private schools) are described, in advance, as an expression of spontaneous popular joy and support.[116] By such shifts are 'forces of development' channelled, tamed and stabilised by the flood barrier of M.I.B., an ideological bulwark whose mere promulgation by the sultan has been declared to be a sufficient condition for its unquestioning acceptance under established tradition.[117]

Now it is germane to note that the 'established tradition' which bestows doctrinal authority is the very same tradition which the doctrine itself aims to perpetuate. There has been a striking metamorphosis, connected with the shift to methodical Islamisation, from the *implied* prescription of descriptive/historical M.I.B. to the explicit imperative of M.I.B. as sultan's will or state policy. 'The tradition' and vested ruling interest are thus nothing if not active in their own support, and while the chief ideologist has invoked the sultan's innate authority in defence of perpetuation, the sultan himself has described the tradition as a divine providence.[118] This 'tightening' of M.I.B. would seem to pose obstacles to economic mobilisation, where at the start of this section we anticipated simply a lack of support from the ideological sphere, and have latterly stressed economic mobilisation under strict control. Obstruction to economic mobilisation would be assured by the values of the simultaneously propagated conservative Islamic revival especially. The only 'saving grace' of an M.I.B. propagated by government officials as a sort of royal command is that its symbolic function, as an index of the officials' own loyalty, may come to overlay behavioural prescription, at least for themselves. That somewhat conjectural possibility will be raised again in Section XVI. For the moment, with regard to youth, it might be unwise to rule out the possibility that the ever greater ambiguity of official calls, as conservative Islamisation is added, may negate their impact on any who sense their ambiguity, apart from evoking a vague, perhaps cynical political loyalty: not a case of energetic mobilisation, certainly - autonomous or controlled - but not altogether one of induced, insidious torpor either.

This section is concluded with a statement which may lay claim to being the most complete and 'correct' ever published on the role of youth in Brunei. The letter won the only prize in an opinions competition for young people, on the set topic 'The youthful students of today are the leaders of tomorrow'. Its perfection is due to its nature as a synthesis in two respects: firstly, of the disconsonant calls for future leadership from below and permanent leadership from above; and secondly, of everything that the sultan and subordinate mouthpieces have ever said on the subject of youth - in other words, a political echo, of no originality, yet by this very token a symptom of ministerial potential in the youthful writer, who truly understands the conditions for future leadership in Brunei Darussalam.

> Youth are the backbone of the State in development. Their every action strengthens the foundation of national development. The majority of youths are involved in education. They are the leaders of tomorrow, and it is only fitting that they should be given this arena in which to equip themselves as helmsmen of the ship of State. This is precisely why the government is always sensitive to the needs of our young people, especially in the field of education. Education gives the primary impetus towards shaping the spirit and character of youth in terms of maximum versatility.

And a new curriculum for all levels, of greater relevance and coherence, is being implemented, that will further enhance the skills of the youthful element in the technical and vocational workforce. A suitable training scheme for youths should also be set up to help prevent them from slipping under the influence of unhealthy social tendencies, for do they not constitute our line of resistance against the moral crisis that is so hotly discussed these days? When that crisis is overcome, how easy it will be for the government to develop the country! The recruitment of young people to fill vacant posts is also expanding. This takes account of the fact that they have the energy to accelerate the national economy in the direction of development.

The formation of associations whose membership is drawn from the younger generation is another means of speeding up national development even more, besides bringing into being youth of high calibre who are dedicated and sensitive to the interests of race and State. Support and encouragement from every walk of life is essential so that our youth become more positive and optimistic in working for development of a more progressive kind.[119]

XII. *The World Outside: The Prevalence of Disorder*

Note has been previously made of the uses of 'Western decadence' as a counterpoint to the purported virtues of Brunei society.[120] At the simplest level, attention is diverted from any objective shortcomings of the latter by pointing up examples of blatant materialism, neglect of the old, and sexual promiscuity in societies of European ethnic stock. Televised religious talks and sermons are the most common medium for this kind of propaganda to the masses (a favourite pulpit parable of the deputy mufti is that of a fertile land which became barren and blighted after a foreigner bathed in its river), and since it is not normally admitted that the blatant examples of immorality are in any way untypical, the approach merges easily with the more general Islamic perspective that the whole of Western society is adrift - not so much because it is *kafir* (infidel) but because it has abandoned religion and become secular.[121] Latterly the sultan has articulated it as an explicit principle of Brunei society that it is *not* 'secular'.[122]

Since Christian missionary activity is execrated as much as secular values, it seems that the taunt that the West has become completely secularised may not be taken quite seriously by those who make it. But in a society where Muslim identity and observance are more vulnerable to 'subversion' by secular influences than by Christian missionaries (who are much easier to keep out), it makes sense for the political authority to focus mainly on the dangers of secularisation. Besides, there may be a genuine belief that *democratic* institutions and ideas are the product of post-Enlightenment secularism in Western culture. Whether valid or not as a historical statement, such a perception would make the need to forestall secularisation look doubly and directly urgent.

However, this is far from being the end of the story as far as the custodians of the 'Bruneian virtues' are concerned. The world that is seen on T.V. screens in Brunei homes is not only one that is propelled in part by secular values, but its politics are commonly (and visibly) in the democratic mould. This creates a need for an actively defensive interpretation of the politics Bruneians see, in order to implant negative evaluations of democracy as far as possible. That the regime perceives such a need is suggested by the discernible functional logic which underlies the diverse strands of official interpretation of external phenomena as a whole and lends the interpretations a greater coherence than may appear at first sight. The overall functional logic is the logic of moral deterrence. The coherence relates to the shared quality of incoherence and louring moral chaos in world affairs, contrasted implicitly or explicitly with the benign calm at the epicentre, Brunei, under its sultan. Not for nothing has the ancient nomenclature for the state been revived: 'Brunei Darussalam' ('The Abode of Peace') - an exemplar of order.

The diffuse and insidious menace of secularism is given more prominence than Christian missionary activity, we have noted. It indeed represents the greater objective danger to traditional socio-political values in Brunei. But the danger of Christianity is an important second strand in official thought and interpretation regarding the world outside and its relations, actual or potential, with local society. In fact, Christianity is more vividly, and thus more credibly, identifiable as a source of threat because of its organised nature; because there have been recent cases of conversion of Muslims to Christianity in Singapore and Malaysia; and because confrontations between the two religions have been tangible and often epic events of history. The idea of a perpetual struggle between opposing, transcendentally defined, blocs offers a way of structuring the international environment which identifies it very effectively as an arena of conflict and danger for Muslims. Brunei is an 'oasis' mercifully isolated from danger for the time being, but only by the grace of Allah and a caring and watchful government. By attributing the security of Islam in Brunei to the present political structure, the ideologues strike a blow, needless to say, for the latter's perpetuation (and deflect any thought that security of religion might create secure conditions for the pursuit of high-level self-interest from within the State itself); but the detailed logical nexus postulated is: devout caliph → security of Islam → God's favour to Brunei → tranquillity of the realm → popular gratitude and loyalty.

Yet the danger to Brunei's tranquillity and Muslim identity from the Christian bloc cannot be illustrated by recalling the British Residency: as argued earlier, the latter involved too much loss of sovereignty and aroused too much anti-monarchical nationalism for comfort, in terms of the tenets of continuity and serenity of royal power respectively. (So it cannot be cited; and if it were, in the context of Christianity, the monarchy would suffer more discredit, especially since the Residency agreement left control of religion with the sultan.) Also, warnings that the Christian world or its front-men, the 'Orientalists', are assiduous in exploiting doctrinal divisions between Muslims, must sound rather abstract or arcane to the average Bruneian.[123] Thus attention is frequently drawn to the Spanish occupation of 1578 with its explicitly imperial and missionary purpose, and the legendary patriotic-cum-royalist-cum-holy uprising of the Brunei Malay people to save themselves from 'rekafirisation'. This was Brunei's only experience of anything like a Crusade, but it was a genuine enough case as far as Spanish motives were concerned. As such, though the reality of a Brunei *jihad* in response may be questioned, this occupation has the value of giving the immediacy of a home-country focus to the Christian menace.[124]

The Spanish occupation does not, however, have the immediacy of topicality in time, i.e. contemporaneity. The regime may even have weakened the force of its warnings about the forward march of Christianity through its policy that the RTB television channel shall never report the activities of the pope, or allow a Christian wedding to be shown in a foreign film. A third strand of thought, 'the International Zionist Plot', has the advantage of immediacy in time but not much by way of a local focal point (the mufti's anathemas against the Brunei Rotary Club in 1984/85 must have fallen flat with most Bruneians, who are not members, and even flatter with the few Malay businessmen who are).[125]

It would thus be perfect for Brunei ideological purposes if an issue could be made of the present conflict between the Christian government and the Muslims (still known as 'Moros', following the old Spanish term) in the southern Philippines. This highly contemporary issue echoes and evokes the 16th-century Hispano-Brunei competition for territory, trade and souls far more strongly than any sermon or historical lecture can ever do, and is also ongoing. However, ASEAN political etiquette forbids 'interference' in the internal affairs of fellow-member states. Therefore the Moros' struggle for autonomy is almost completely banished from the RTB. (Even an oblique portrayal of the Mount Pinatubo eruption as a manifestation of divine wrath, in two weather bulletins during June 1991, had to be dropped when winds carried volcanic ash out from the non-Muslim Philippines and deposited some of it on cars in Muslim Brunei!). So far as the Filipino case can serve any didactic purpose for Brunei society, it has generally had to be absorbed into a fourth strand of thought on the international environment: the category of the many Third World states which, through Western imperialism and partial assimilation of Western political values, have succumbed to the turbulence of democracy.

This is not to say that there can be specific comment on the endemic political turbulence of Brunei's neighbour. But its proximity makes it an object of spontaneous popular interest. Thus it was possible for RTB to dwell at length on the overthrow of President Marcos in 1986 in the certainty of an eager and attentive audience. In the first stages the uprising and bloodshed presumably served, in official Brunei calculation, to illustrate the upheavals that go with democracy. But nor did the authorities seem to lack confidence, after the dictator had fallen and fled, that most Bruneians would draw the 'correct' lesson from revelations of abuses of power by the Marcos family: not that absolute power corrupts absolutely (as many expatriates in Brunei felt, perceiving immediate and glaring parallels between the Marcos clan and the Brunei Royal Family), but that it is characteristically democracy that gives rise to dictators who plunder a nation's wealth. Here, again, the world outside is to be seen as a zone of turmoil, but the dangers for Brunei in this kind of case come not in the form of aggression but of unhealthy models of political development. Still, such states were themselves subject to the aggression of prolonged colonialism in their time, and democracy is the legacy of colonialism. Obliquely, democratic turbulence is a function of the historical phenomenon of imperialist aggression.

From all such misfortunes, according to official doctrine, Brunei has been spared until now. The one exception - the flirtation with democratic violence known as 'the Brunei Rebellion' - was quickly put down by the benign force of monarchy combined with Islam, which constitutes its transcendental inspiration as well as the ideology of the State.[126] As for future colonisation by a Western power, the Brunei government does not speak of this as an imminent prospect. But it does maintain - by way of a fifth strand in its international view - that the turbulence of this world of democratic nation states could spill over into aggression against a small and vulnerable state like Brunei. Now an interesting and very recent sub-strand of this idea (a further case of ideology adapting to environment), posits a desire by external interests to destabilise Brunei through hostile propaganda, because they are jealous of what it has achieved through political unity. But this threat is vaguely associated with the Western media and seems more akin to subversion by secularism. Presumably the source of any literal aggression would be some other regional state (though ASEAN etiquette again intervenes to forbid the expression of such anxiety, and least of all is it possible to suggest to the Brunei public that a Muslim neighbour might be the source). Thus Brunei puts great faith, publicly, in organisations of collective security: the United Nations first and foremost; the Commonwealth; and also ASEAN.

This is in fact its official foreign policy posture, not a case of mere ideological 'construction' of the international environment projected to the public for purposes of legitimation.[127] Unfortunately, not one of the three international organisations or groupings mentioned has the nature of a military alliance. Their power for defensive action is only as strong as the resolve of their strongest members to act - and often in a framework other than that of the organisation itself, which may be precluded from military action. In the case of ASEAN, militarisation has been excluded for the whole of its history since 1967, because the fragile comity of interest which binds the members has been believed capable of succumbing at any moment to the pressures of individual national self-interest. This highlights once again the fact that Brunei's regional environment is the more obvious source of any future threat to its independence.

Brunei's response to this predicament has been to seek countervailing assurance from a more distant and powerful state, which yet has no interest in (or capacity to exert) a dominating influence. There is a historical precedent in Brunei's relations with the Ming Dynasty of China, but today the strategic partner and possible protector in a future hour of need is of 'the West': the United Kingdom, the very state whose protective shield the sultanate was so reluctant to lose in the 1970s and whose continuing involvement potentially calls in question the credentials of the Brunei regime as a preserver of independence. Does a British military role not suggest a need for the kind of nationalist revival which the regime has always declared redundant to Brunei's needs? Despite repeated insinuation that the Gurkha Battalion is a part of the sultan's own forces,[128] most Bruneians surely still know otherwise. The fact that unfriendly construction can very easily be placed on the British link may well explain the emergence of a powerful sixth strand of 'international thought' in official communication with the public.

This sixth strand harks back to the second, but instead of focusing on the danger of Christian expansion to Brunei itself, expresses a strong stand in support of Third World independence movements further afield. (So far as such independence movements lack any element of Muslim nationalism, this strand postulates the continuing existence of general Western imperialism in the world, without a missionary dimension.) But there are not, of course, many such movements left, and the attractive cause of one or another ethnic minority cannot be espoused because these tend to be directed against states whose boundaries and sovereignty, like Brunei's, enjoy the shelter of

U.N. principles (or in the case of the Filipino government under siege in the southern islands, the protection of ASEAN too). But the two 'pariah states' of South Africa and Israel, subject to much U.N. sanction and resolution, and not on Brunei's diplomatic list, seem to make a useful exception to the rule. Thus, with the authority of the sultan's U.N. speech,[129] the Brunei foreign affairs ministry and the government media have conducted, across these few years, a persistent if relatively low-key campaign against 'the Pretoria regime' and 'the Tel Aviv regime', in favour of the human rights of black South Africans and Muslim Palestinians. In spite of international ostracism of these two states, the implicit confidence that Brunei's actions do not create an uncomfortable precedent for interference in the internal affairs of sovereign states, including protest against racial discrimination, imprisonment without trial and denial of electoral rights (on each of which issues Brunei itself might be thought a vulnerable target), seems not without interest.[130] (Before passing on we must not fail to observe that the sultanate loses no opportunity to intimate to its subjects that the ceremonial expressions of respect to the head of state which accompany diplomatic relations under the 'post-Congress of Vienna system' convey not merely recognition of the sultanate's territorial power as a *fact*, but also respect for the sultan in a personal sense and a legitimating acknowledgment of the *value* of Brunei's political institutions. Indeed the international state system has it uses! So far the sultanate has operated within it almost entirely on its own, beneficial terms.)

Meanwhile, the issue of the holy places of Islam under Israeli occupation lends concrete confirmation to the theme of a Zionist plot against Islam. The American role in support of Israel provides further linkage between Zionism and general Western imperialism. With the help of television, the Palestinian uprising has given RTB an extended 'field day', needless to say, based on video footage supplied by the - officially despised - Western news agencies. The imprisonment of Nelson Mandela was also an emotive issue which RTB exploited to the full - though it nearly backfired when his sudden release all but handed the world record for length of political imprisonment to Brunei.[131] And one function of these emotive issues, it may be suggested, is to project the modern world, lastly, as an arena not merely of turbulence but of suffering: this in distinction from both the tranquillity and the welfare which Brunei enjoys, free from the slightest tinge of foreign influence, let alone imperialism. From this contrast the excellence of the Brunei sultanate as a defender of its realm and people is more than inferred. But far more importantly, both the humanitarian and *nationalist* credentials of the sultanate are affirmed - yet without any practical, destabilising consequences for its regional environment, nor, indirectly (by spill-over or revengeful counteraction), for its own political structure, since the two 'pariah states' are remote from Southeast Asia. Indeed the government achieves the useful objective of diverting popular attention from both its own human rights record and its rather 'contra'-nationalist defence arrangements.[132] Considering that British foreign policy has been several degrees to the 'right' of most Third World sentiment on both South Africa and Israel, the need to divert attention from the defence arrangement with Britain is particularly manifest; but it may attest to the Brunei government's sang-froid that precisely the South African and Palestinian issues are used for such ends, as it substitutes a diversionary, surrogate nationalism for the autochthonous version.

From a standpoint in mid-1990 it would have been incautious to try to hazard how far the Brunei government's tactic, if such it consciously was, was based on a correct calculation of 'consumer reaction'. A year later, however, with the Gulf War now fought and receding into history, it is possible to make a quite empirical assessment of the impact of the sultanate's 'nationalism for distant shores'. The Gulf War afforded an opportunity for the government to combine the pro-nationalist strand of its international thought with the theme of resistance to a neo-Crusade. The opportunity was duly taken - though not without the subtlety of maintaining for diplomatic purposes a solidarity of sorts with the anti-Iraq coalition.

XIII. The World Outside: The Gulf War

To some extent the pro-Iraqi position of the media during the war was dictated by their own exploitation of the Palestinian issue in previous years and by the broader anti-Christian and anti-Zionist strands in official constructions of the international environment. The public was already in a high state of suggestibility in relation to any pro-Palestinian appeal. The widespread acceptance of Saddam Hussein at face value as the saviour of the Palestinians, within all strata, thus finds a ready explanation, and the government would have been ill-advised to stand aside from such sentiment.

This anti-Western climate was further fostered by the Malay press of Malaysia in the count-down to war,[133] while RTB took the American anti-war movement no less seriously than Saddam appears to have done, and helped to plant a fundamental disbelief in the possibility of war - with the corollary that if it did break out, President Bush would be cast in the role of 'sole responsible criminal war-monger' by virtue of ignoring 'the wishes of peace-loving Americans' as well as 'the aspirations of Muslims'. As for the local English-language newspaper, now controlled by the foreign minister through his company, QAF Holdings, the thrust of its weekly opinion column was simultaneously to discount the possibility of war and to warn that President Bush's dangerous bluff and 'verbal mud-slinging' against the 'dignified President Saddam' could lead to a disaster, more especially for America's own interests.[134] Perhaps not coincidentally, many Brunei Muslims succumbed to a mood which actually wanted a war so that the Americans would be taught a bloody lesson in a 'new Vietnam'. The consequent frustration and fury when this did not happen are understandable.

It is less easy to understand, however, how large numbers of any Muslim nation could contrive to overlook or discount the original rape of Kuwait as a blow to the 'aspirations of Muslims' and their corresponding human rights, however deplorable the consequent arrival of American forces in Saudi Arabia might be from a Muslim perspective. This has proved an intractable puzzle to many non-Muslims during the recent crisis: it is a question which has been asked world-wide, not simply with reference to Brunei. But with particular reference to Brunei it beggared belief for most expatriate observers in the country that Bruneians should not empathise with Kuwait on grounds of similar political structure, oil wealth and territorial extent. If they were hostile to royal absolutism, then indifference or even hostility to Kuwait would be proper and in the logic of their political outlook, but there has not been the faintest suggestion of a republican dimension to Bruneian support for Saddam and hatred for the Western allies. The irresistible, underlying political values in the case have proved to be the twin principles that while a war between Muslim brothers is merely deplorable, military intervention by *kafir* states against one of those brethren is utterly damnable (with or without the added element of 'Americans defecating on holy soil', as one UBD student put it). These values obviously lie deeper than anything that could be attributed to a couple of years' exposure to the sight of Palestinian youths and Israeli troops exchanging stones and tear gas in the Occupied Territories.

However, in the immediate count-down, the lack of any film from inside Kuwait, and RTB's eager use of any material from Baghdad, must have reinforced popular suggestibility. Moreover there was a noticeable lack of any attempt to educate the Brunei public on 'the evil of Saddam', despite official support for the U.N. resolutions. While the foreign minister's speech at the U.N. General Assembly on 3 October 1990 cited the invasion of Kuwait as an object lesson on the vulnerability of small states,[135] an accompanying commentary on Brunei's foreign policy by the chief propaganda writer of the information department avoided any reference to the Middle East crisis.[136] Three weeks later, on the other hand, the latter contributed a rousing essay on the epic bravery of the gentle Palestinians.[137] The sultan's New Year message made a reference to Kuwait as the victim of the greed of a large power, but also, with more emphasis, seemed to suggest that the Kuwaitis had 'asked for trouble' because of political disunity (read: 'disloyalty to the monarch'?) and complacency. There is no way of knowing the precise intended meaning of the allusion, since in any case Kuwait was never made the subject of one of *Pelita Brunei*'s didactic editorials.[138]

At any rate, by the time the United Nations deadline expired, there was 'no other way but forward' for the Brunei media, if the media were not to lose the sympathy of their listeners, viewers and readers - that is, the way already pointed and pioneered by the same media and the religious establishment for some time past. But perhaps much more to the point, there was even considerable advantage to be gained from a judiciously pro-Iraqi posture, whatever may have gone before.

The advantage on offer was basically two-sided. On the one hand, once Saddam had stepped forward as a fighter for Islam (both by announcing himself as the saviour of the Palestinians and by portraying himself the victim of a Western-led coalition), to be seen as his friend would benefit the standing of almost any Muslim regime with its own populace. But in Brunei's own special circumstances, on the other hand, the value of Saddam's purportedly pro-Palestinian motives was precisely that he thereby diverted attention from the 'real issue' as seen by the alliance (and understood perfectly well by the Brunei government): the annexation of Kuwait. For the Western allies, taking their stand on the 'noble principle' of the inviolability of national borders, it was still a source of discomfort that into the bargain they were having to rescue an 'anachronistic Muslim autocracy'. But for the Brunei sultanate, itself a Muslim autocracy, even to say a lot on the issue of national sovereignty was fraught with risks, because to focus on the fate of Kuwait from any aspect at all could direct attention to the fact that it was specifically a Muslim autocracy, almost identical to the sultanate, that was subject to the rescue operation, and with exactly the kind of infidel strategic consortium in the leading role that underpins Brunei's political structure. Potentially, Saddam's diversionary tactic did not go far enough for Brunei, for he also sought inconveniently to justify the annexation in its own right as a blow struck for the Arab poor!

However, the risks of a pro-Saddam posture being exposed as self-interested, contradictory hypocrisy were probably felt to be minimal because of the overriding emotional power and consequent 'redibility' of the call for a pro-Palestinian and anti-Western *jihad*, and because most Bruneians are slow to conceptualise intellectual consistency, or the possibility of bad faith at higher levels, at least in the sultan himself. Ignorance of the dynamics of international politics, of networks of strategic and economic interest, and of systems of high-tech warfare would probably ensure that most Bruneians (and observation suggests that this applies to many of the educated too) would never begin to conceive that Brunei might already be locked into these systems itself. As for the credibility of Saddam's claim to be fighting for the Palestinians, there was some safety for the Brunei government (if it took Saddam's side) in the fact that most Bruneians have little clear impression of where Iraq is, at least in relation to the Israel which Saddam was preparing to 'destroy'. (These aspects could be known or foreseen by the government.) A further, and very positive, consideration in favour of tacit government support for Saddam was that this new Gulf War was being fought by a Sunni Muslim. Even if Saddam was only a nominal Muslim by all the evidence of his previous conduct, his charisma could usefully serve to wean Bruneian affections away from the Shi'a Iran to which they had been attracted in the Iran-Iraq war. Lastly, an 'Islamic' stand accorded perfectly with the government's current shift towards greater rigour in religion at home and its concern to avoid being outflanked by Al-Arqam.

At all events, RTB, as a department under the prime minister's office, left no doubt of the government's position (however 'unofficial') once war began. The sudden switch to a strong anti-Western line in the TV news jolted even casual foreign viewers who normally show little interest in politics. At first, tendentious RTB commentary was combined with a mass of uncensored agency reporting whose message was balanced and often inconsistent with what RTB had to say. But after four days or so, the news editors 'got their act together' and cut out most of the agency sound. There was a strong preference for Western agency material collected inside Iraq, RTB forbearing to point out either that the material was subject to censorship by the Iraqi authorities or that Iraqi claims of massive damage to civilian areas and loss of civilian life were usually not attested by the actual pictorial evidence shown. The American and allied case got far too little exposure to compete for attention, let alone sympathy. For several weeks after the war's precipitate end, RTB's star editor continued to fight a 'rearguard action' for Saddam, portraying him as: the victim of unethical, high-tech weaponry, whose use by the allies was comparable to the atomic bombing of Hiroshima in World War II (and was to be the subject of a War Crimes Tribunal in the United States); the man who had wanted to withdraw from Kuwait but was not given a fair chance (and now faces unproven allegations that his troops blew up Kuwait's oil wells when they did withdraw); the leader who stands high in his people's affections, even after *they* were punished for *his* error (an annexation which in any case was insignificant beside the Jews' long 'annexation of Palestine'); the Arab who deserves the confidence of the Kurds.[139]

The director of information and broadcasting parried informal diplomatic complaints during the war weeks with the claim that RTB's success in maintaining balance could be judged from the fact that he was receiving many complaints from Bruneians about the station's 'pro-American bias'. At the same time, spokesmen of the foreign affairs ministry were letting it be known, 'off the record', that they were unhappy about RTB's line, so contrary to the ministry's stand at the United Nations, yet every word of advice and admonition had fallen (they maintained) on deaf ears.

It should be noted, however, that while Brunei supported the resolutions and several times condemned the annexation of Kuwait, it also implied by the force of its regrets at the outbreak of war in January and the 'escalation' in February that negotiation and a political solution were the only course of action that it could accept.[140] Diplomats were not slow to note the paradox that, in contrast to official protestations of antipathy towards Saddam, the newspaper with the 'hot-line' connection to the foreign affairs ministry was actually taking a stronger line than RTB. This was evinced in part by a general preference for reports of bombing by the allies in the selection of news agency items, and the use of slanted headlines. But more than anything else one would wish to commemorate the writer of a weekly commentary on world affairs who, for partisan vitriol, took more than a page from the 'twisted outpourings of the chauvinist Western-controlled media' which he claimed to have identified and desired to discredit.[141] That the writer in question enjoys clearance at the highest possible level could be surmised from the fact of a fairly sensitive piece on Limbang which appeared in the same issue of the *Bulletin* as his vituperative correspondence column retort to an angry expatriate over the Gulf War.[142]

Also enjoying high-level clearance, but in a rather different way, was the pro-Saddam material entering the country from Malaysia. To understand the significance of official indulgence towards this material, it is important to appreciate the normal rigour of Brunei censorship. The authorities are on their guard for anything that might tend to excite political sentiment. The majority of cases involve short reports of royal activity abroad, or of government policy, or of PRB statements, which from the unique perspective of the government of Brunei seem disrespectful or unduly informative. Not surprising, then, that weightier writings attract hostile attention. By way of recent example: an inflammatory Malay sermon on Salman Rushdie in the Malaysian tri-weekly *Watan* was excised;[143] no less, a rambling excursion into popular theology on the theme of 'Evil' in *Time*;[144] while the latest edition of a general history of Malaysia, Singapore and Brunei, which includes a new statement that the various military units in Brunei are 'designed more for internal security than external defence', came under ban in March 1991 and can no longer be read even at UBD.[145] It is in this light that the admission of pro-Saddam writings which are equally or far more inflammatory in tone constitutes a striking contrast to normal policy - not just because of their touch of religious fanaticism but because they virtually incite to violence against Western interests.[146]

But in the end it was the depiction of the bombed air raid shelter in Baghdad that aroused the strongest feelings among the Brunei public. Again the significance of the decision to make use of this material has to be judged in the light of normal RTB policy, which does not uphold freedom of information but seeks to avoid showing anything that might in the slightest way discredit or contradict government policy and official perceptions of the world. (This is why RTB television bulletins are usually so full of plane crashes and ferry disasters from remote corners of the globe: these items are politically neutral!) That the government was willing to allow emotions to be stirred on this occasion received ample confirmation when the sultan in his National Day speech rejected any military actions affecting cities and populated areas of Iraq, in furtherance of the United Nations resolutions.[147] That the sultan is aware that the aims of the resolutions could not have been achieved without neutralising Iraqi command centres and establishing air superiority, and that civilian casualties are part and parcel of modern warfare, can hardly be doubted in view of his own Sandhurst background and current enthusiasm for building up Brunei's jet fighter force, not to mention the ground-to-air missile battery already in place and manned by British personnel. Who will doubt, indeed, that as of 23 February the government was assuming that precisely this normal pattern of air warfare would continue, as a necessary reinforcement to the ground offensive while the latter got under way? Anticipating further civilian casualties and mounting popular anger in Brunei, the sultan's protest merely showed common political prudence. But his position was consistent with the spirit of earlier calls for 'a political solution' at all costs.

In fact Brunei's foreign policy declarations have always inferred the existence of an adequate *moral* power of international organisations to solve international conflict, *without resort to force*. Without doubt such a stand will have helped to divert attention from Brunei's own involvement in the 'sordid' world of military pacts. Yet the 'moral force' idea seemed to have acquired a life of its own and a certain power over the sultan's perceptions where he made his sensational call for actions by peace activists all over the world to stop the war, and berated the 'futile' United Nations for its failure to prevent it in the first place through diplomacy.[148] The embarrassment of having to greet Kuwait's liberation within days[149] - with overtones of cynicism after so firmly rejecting the means of its realisation - can never have been anticipated. But even with foresight the sultan's posture would have been prescribed to some extent, in the light of existing doctrine as well as awareness of the trend of public opinion.

The great asset of the Brunei government that has become apparent from the Gulf War is that the majority of Bruneians today, including even the most thoughtful among the intelligentsia (those to whom one might look for political criticism internally, and eventual action), face a profound difficulty or 'blockage' in imagining that Brunei could ever be attacked by a Muslim neighbour (even though Brunei faced military infiltration by Indonesia as recently as the 1960s and a hostile diplomatic campaign by Malaysia until the late 1970s); or that, consequently, Brunei would ever see military actions undertaken on its behalf by a non-Muslim ally against 'Muslim' cities. There is also a related substantial blockage today regarding the possibility of British counter-insurgency in support of the sultan. Consequently Brunei's defence links with the United Kingdom are losing their capacity to excite animosity or foreboding. Although the official construction of the international environment does not exclude, among its strands, the possibility of regional aggression or 'trouble-making' by infiltrated elements, possibly in league with the foreign media, the more telling emphasis has clearly been on the fact that the major conflicts of our time take place in more distant parts and represent the epic, almost timeless struggle between forces of darkness (Western imperialism, Christianity) and forces of light (national independence, Islam). In this framework it has proved possible for the sultanate to be seen to side with 'the light' in the Gulf War and not be compromised by any trace of association with 'darkness'. And by complementary definition, why should Brunei ever be attacked by any 'Muslim brother' state (or the sultan be attacked by 'fellow Muslim' Bruneians)? At the same time, the sheer physical distance between Brunei and the Gulf seems to confirm Brunei as a haven of peace under its benevolent and patriotic ruler. By way of constructive utilisation of the existing ideological dispositions in society (partly of the government's own creation though they may be)[150] the government has even been able to insinuate that Brunei has a contribution to make to the world's liberation from oppression and suffering, purely by admonition and without the slightest implication that struggle or revolution are suited to the condition of Brunei itself. (Not even anti-American or anti-British demonstrations can be permitted under the Brunei State of Emergency, yet the sultan's call for demonstrations in other countries, far from exposing inconsistency, seems able to *divert* questions of the type: "What internal 'danger' is it that forces the sultan to rule through emergency powers and forbid political expression at home?")

Nevertheless, by working within the already established framework and direction of a broadly 'Islamic' response to world events, the government has done much to consolidate the same ideological and emotional 'mind-set' among the Malay population. This inevitably narrows the options for any alternative direction in future. So far from maintaining distance from the outer world, that 'zone of chaos and suffering', the government has brought it much nearer and has actually encouraged popular identification with the 'Muslim oppressed'. The war has revealed, and roused, a still latent streak of nationalism in Brunei Malay society, which though basically chauvinist and anti-Western in its current expression, could bode ill for stability if its focus were to become more localised.

In other words, although the war did not last long enough to provoke demonstrations or violent actions against Western interests in Brunei (and even though the cynosure of Muslims in the war was of the Sunni sect), the government must now live with a more sensitised people, whose new mental condition indicates the need for further adaptation on the government's side. On the one hand there is little alternative to more emphasis on religion in general. But on the other hand, it is imperative that the potential radicalism of identification with the 'Muslim oppressed', and any revival of class thinking, whether à la Arqam or PRB-style, be pre-empted by explicitly conservative forms of Islamisation.

That the government has already taken stock of its post-war situation in some such terms is strongly suggested by the announcement of a government-sponsored fund for Bangladesh cyclone victims. The announcement, by the sultan himself on 18 May 1991 and echoed in a major sermon on charity,[151] has claimed the fund as an expression of 'universalism' and a 'Muslim moral imperative'. This will seem an eminently worthy and unobjectionable call from most points of view. But it is notable that the government of Brunei, unlike the government of Malaysia in relation to the Palestinian liberation struggle or the war in Afghanistan, has never previously ventured to collect funds and thereby cultivate or legitimate popular identification with Muslim issues overseas. The choice of a non-political cause for this very first public donation may denote the recognition both of a heightened awareness of world issues outside the 'charmed circle', and of a need to channel it into harmless by-ways. (That an international charity effort may help to teach Bruneians that they are relatively well-off is of course a bonus.) But even in the theory of Bruneian international charity there is reference to moral competition with the non-Islamic world,[152] while in particular an unusually politicised sermon on Palestine prompts the question whether the government is now entirely free to designate the agenda when seeking to generate popular support through international issues.[153]

It is on this questioning note that we turn now to survey aspects of the royal monopoly of State revenues and reserves: another area in which the government's room for ideological manoeuvre might seem to be objectively limited, and grass-roots emotion only too prone to get out of hand. Whatever its assets in the form of international diversions, the government needs reserves of political skill in conjuring a 'nation' in a context of private control of would-be public revenue.

XIV. Towards a Conclusion: Royal Wealth or Common Weal?

It was concluded towards the end of Section XI that the sultanate in its collective wisdom had decided that divine right stood to over-stimulate 'tender minds' less than a theory of social contract might do. But in one way or another, does not any intensively propagated ideology invite its consumers to think? Most will be guided by the ideology, but some - amidst all the other stimuli of economic and cultural change - could be moved to think for themselves. An ideology whose descriptive statements are broadly divergent from common-sense perception of reality, or from alternative information, or indeed from other, simultaneous statements of the ideology itself, would surely create a minor crisis of credibility among a literate citizenry. When the purpose behind the ideology is to cultivate or preserve values which most other political cultures at a comparable level of socio-economic development have rejected (as where, most typically of all and for a fee, 'the Richest Man in the World' is declared to rule 'by God's Will'), ideological propagation might of itself suggest a crisis of consolidation in a regime defending a newly emergent form of monopolistic interest - not least because *divine* favour is so strongly invoked. This is a possibility that must at least be considered, the more so if policy were seen to be promoting vested interest in ways not even foreshadowed by doctrine.

To the present writer, at least, the most unintentionally 'revealing' propositions of the Bruneian ideology are the boast that Brunei did not allow the British to break trust with the monarchy or impose their cultural influence as they did vis-à-vis the sultanates of the peninsula,[154] and the associated normative stand that what 'survived' through the era of colonialism is worth preserving for ever and ever. But this paper has already said enough to show that initial British intervention in Brunei's administration had aims almost opposite to 'preserving' an existing tradition. There was no sign of a powerful and wealthy monarchy in 1905. The Brunei *kerajaan* was rebuilt from a territorially decentralised, exploiting yet impoverished, if not mainly ceremonial, realm into a centralised, bureaucratic, revenue-controlling State in the modern mould. And the physical starting point - what was 'preserved' - was a rump of territory, the residue from a century of attrition, the bare trace of a foothold on the island of Borneo that would enable Sultan Hashim's line to maintain its credibility as a 'ruling dynasty'.

Thus far, the differences from the peninsular States may be mainly differences of degree, as to the impoverishment and decentralisation of power which faced the British at the beginning of their intervention, and the relatively greater transformation experienced by Brunei (in relation to its previous weakness, that is). However, after 1959, instead of transferring control of the reconstructed Brunei realm to something even newer - an elected government - the British acted in a highly exaggerated (and in the Malay world, unprecedented) spirit of would-be obligation to 'the lawful heirs of the body of Sultan Hashim'. Colonial indirect rule was suddenly superseded by absolute monarchy. It is precisely the novelty of this new-found power - and later, extreme wealth - besides the lack of regional analogues, that necessitated claims of structural continuity by the late sultan and his coterie. Admittedly, concern with dynastic continuity, at least, has a long history. But concern is a rather insubstantial form of 'continuity' (especially if one considers Sultan Hashim a 'newcomer', not being the son of the previous sultan), and may not suggest more than that dynastic vulnerability and the *will* for power in its changing forms are constants.[155]

Now while the sultanate has to apply cosmetic surgery to the fissures in its historical countenance, it is also true that democracy in the peninsular Malay States constitutes a break with Malay tradition. But the question is justified: is the neo-traditional monarchical absolutism of Brunei really more viable than the peninsular Malay constitutional monarchies with *their* 'British legacy', upholding a form of democracy and being partly legitimated by it, free from the imperative to write a suspect ideological script in their own behalf? Inevitably also, the existence of the constitutional Malay monarchies so close at hand offers a visible alternative model of political development for Bruneians to contemplate, not to speak of the associated, vigorous life of nationalist politics that has transformed the peninsular Malays, despite some costs. (The costs include the plural society itself: ironically a precondition of Malay transformation and of reasonably objective ideology, but also a potentially repellant aspect of the Malaysian model for Bruneians, as we have seen.)

From one point of view, the greatest gift of Great Britain to the Brunei monarchy, by design or default - next to the Constitution itself - was the 25 years' respite between the Constitution and 'full independence,' which enabled it to consolidate its political hegemony and sundry forms of access to oil income, while nationalist eyes were still turned accusingly towards the protecting power. The greatest betrayal, correspondingly, as the late

Seri Begawan Sultan well foresaw, was the withdrawal of protection and the effective camouflage which it had furnished to dynastic power, compelling the sultanate now to come to terms with its own subjects on an 'early modern' basis, i.e. to call on them to think of themselves as a 'nation', as well as identifying the sultanate as a heritage shared with the dynasty. In turn, the concept of a nation (even when rendered by *negara*, meaning 'the State', with monarchical overtones), and the conception of youth as agents of development (even when hedged with the proviso that only the State defines its aims and modalities), invite citizens to think about issues such as control of 'national wealth'. It is popular anxieties about financial abuse, more than any desire for elections, that are beginning to direct critical attention towards divine right and other claims of official doctrine. This is happening even before the propagation of ideology as such begins to arouse suspicions of moral vulnerability. (And suspicion seems the more likely where critical ideas themselves are prompting an even more active propagation of divine right.)

It does therefore seem conceivable that, in the end, the monarchy's control of wealth may prove to be its Achilles Heel - the most ambiguous bequest of British protection, more dangerous than the withdrawal of protection itself. At the same time, the ideological approach to legitimation, which seems so necessary because of an underlying sense of vulnerability as a new economic interest - or because, paradoxically, the enormous power bequeathed by the British forecloses the democratic option - has a potential to weaken public legitimacy further by overstrengthening a private conviction of right, and of financial prerogative, within the regime itself. Such surmises are mainly prompted by an increasing royal insouciance, if not cynicism, in the practice of double standards at a time of drastic cuts in the public budget and paralysis in government payments to small contractors. Even the debilitating investment in grandiose military infrastructure may be as functional to personal vanity as to objective strategic requirements.

The present study has not referred to any arguments defending royal control and consumption of wealth. This is not due to an oversight. In this context - even more than in other financial matters (Finance Minister Prince Jefri is the only minister who never makes a public speech) - the regime seems to regard silence as the better part of valour. However, statements are becoming more common - and special disbursements too - which focus on the existence of a private royal fortune and thereby imply that it is quite separate from the state reserves. Attempts are made to give it an aura of 'historical respectability' and make it look genuinely private by giving the public to understand that it was 'the Seri Begawan's bequest'.[156]

Nothing illustrates better the rise of royal self-perception as a class than this awareness of an imperative to belie the fact that the State and state reserves are the monarchy's instrument and property respectively. Ironically, in admitting to an enormous private fortune, the monarchy also admits the distinctive concept of a 'public purse'. At the same time, however, developmental doctrine still lends tacit support to a quasi-traditional understanding that the national wealth lies within the sultan's sole prerogative to administer, at least in the form of government services for which popular gratitude is due as to a bestower of gifts. Or the right to control the national wealth is subsumed as an unspoken, complementary tenet within the doctrine of absolute (but just and beneficent) monarchy, while personal expenditure by the royal family is quite well protected from comment by the taboo on *lèse majesté*, which the privileged bureaucratic elite has a common interest with the monarchy in maintaining.

But the ruling interest has yet to resolve the contradiction between its class behaviour as expressed through royal prerogative, and official calls to stop vandalism and 'respect public property'. There is no complete security in the fact that nation-building and the definition of the Bruneian political identity are initiated and promoted 'from the top down'. The concepts of 'common weal', of a 'social contract', and the 'rise of a nation'[157] mark additions to the ideological repertoire which may give a little impetus to development activity but also direct attention towards how the national wealth as a whole is spent. The latest pledge to attend to the needs of the lowest-paid - as the youthful base of the population pyramid, and youth unemployment, swell - is far from diverting attention from the existence of an incipient 'social question'.[158]

XV. Prospects: The Chances of Change

There may be some who are ready to shed a tear of commiseration for an 'ancient polity' placed on the defensive by the encroachments of modernisation. Such is the sentiment which Lord Chalfont wishes to impart. But there is no analogy between the contemporary Brunei State and a powerless Bornean tribe facing extinction. Modern Brunei is a product of the modern age *par excellence*, a state which could very easily have disappeared as a distinct and sovereign entity in 1905 or 1963, but since it did not, is now equipped with the political and economic means to argue that the twentieth century brought no changes at all. But the capacity to conjure an unchanging past is not equivalent to the power to make time, henceforth, stand still. On the contrary - and still in the spirit of the previous section - one might be disposed to predict that conservative religious teachings, while forestalling demands for political participation, will also inhibit the changes of attitude needed for economic development. Indirectly, then, political discontent would be fortified, though diverted by religion in the short term. At the same time an overdose of ideology may well produce symptoms of 'resistance' in the more educated segments of the body politic, even if the doctor fails to recognise the signs of it, being increasingly 'addicted' to his own drug. This is merely to say that the dynasty seems set to vest considerable confidence in its ideologues both native and mercenary, and to be increasingly convinced of the efficacy - even the veracity - of what they say; but should this cause existing patterns of royal behaviour, politically and economically, to be consolidated, while the impact of ideology on the public mind shows diminishing returns, then indeed ideological effort will have proved counterproductive.[159]

In the absence of an early armed forces coup, but paving the way for one later, the worst scenario for the royal family in the next half-decade would be a coalescence of two kinds of discontent. Both are connected with the potentially declining credibility of State ideology, but the focus here is on two elements, specifically defined: firstly, educated younger Bruneians drawn to religion initially through State-funded Islamic propagation itself, but applying an Islamic critique to the sultan, under the influence of Arqam, as the credibility of his purportedly transcendental qualities and divine commission wears thin; secondly, secular technocrats who perceive that the breathing space for economic development which M.I.B. was supposed to have afforded (by keeping fundamentalism at bay) has seen no rise in any indices except for royal investment, income and expenditure.

Now it happens that a handful of idealistic modernists place hope precisely in Islamic revival as a source of ultimate economic resurgence. But viewing all restraints of the Brunei situation, including the conservatism of the increasingly dominant Islamic establishment and the ever more transcendental prescriptions of M.I.B., one may feel sceptical. As Islamisation advances, a lurking suspicion crystallises into a hypothesis for foreign observers that, in the eyes of royalty, even economic development (via the current plan for industrialisation) is fraught with too many participatory disadvantages to outweigh its potentially stabilising effects. On the side of the secularist economic planners, therefore, where the strengthening of the conservative religious establishment was not only a price that seemed worth paying, for keeping radical fundamentalism in check, but, by a far greater irony, may even have been advocated in order to stabilise society while industrialisation provides employment for youth, modernises the Brunei popular mentality and ultimately *weakens* the hold of religion, the chances of satisfaction are particularly questionable.[160]

Moreover, while in general the concessions to Islam in Brunei's social life and education are an unsavoury pill for the secular technocrats, both civilian and military, to swallow, there is also some alienation within the upper Pengiran stratum - the hereditary aristocracy - where Islamisation tends to be seen as a power-play and distortion of Brunei-Malay tradition on the part of the non-hereditary nobility, the Pehins. If, then, the economic benefits of stability are confined to the royal rentier economy, while more generally stabilisation through M.I.B. fosters stagnation, the door should be truly open to a critical analysis of the functions of ideology in Brunei's political system. At that point, the continued promotion of M.I.B. by the State would have become, contrary to its aim of unification, a factor for division between a narrow ruling group and a coalition of other interests - a coalition seeking, in effect, to write a new chapter in Brunei history, and deny, by implication, the thesis that the 'recovery of full independence' by and for an absolute monarchy in 1984 was a mere footnote to an epic of continuity, rather than a landmark in a more than usually discontinuous and 'deviated' process of historical transformation.

In fact, in the late 1980s a more immediate danger than disunity within lay in the effect of royal investments overseas in igniting the unquenchable enmity of a British business genius with a not inconsiderable penchant for the written word. As the year 1990 dawned, the Brunei public found itself confronted with a choice of propaganda for the first time in fifteen years, if not a quarter of a century, and thus a new stimulus to viewing State doctrine with scepticism. The mass distribution of collaborative Lonrho and PRB materials[161] followed shortly upon the fall of dictatorships in Eastern Europe, and PRB called upon the sultan to move with the trend.[162] The new decade seemed to promise much interest for the student of political ideas and their multi-directional interplay with political structure and world events. Of more fascination than all other issues was whether self-protective ideology, that characteristic perquisite of modern power, would prove to have acted as a 'self-destruct mechanism' within, and for, Southeast Asia's 'historic deviation', rather than consolidating a 'new class'; and whether, ultimately, there are generic patterns of regional history from which no deviation can be more than a passing ripple.

XVI. Prospects: The Chances of Continuity

All this was in the 'logic' of the Brunei situation as seen by the present observer as the foundations of the study were laid between mid-1989 and mid-1990. It was a 'logic' that encompassed a ruling family whose interests, both political and economic, were difficult to reconcile, beyond the short term, with those of a rapidly growing population; it included the dimension of scepticism and resistance towards official doctrine as educated Bruneians came to analyse this 'output' in terms of a 'functionality' prejudicial to themselves and nearly all other groups; it incorporated a predicted sense of betrayal among economic planners as they saw even their quite conservative vision diverted or denied; and lastly it took into account the rise of external sources of propaganda and encouragement (both religious and secular) for political change.

Unfortunately, one other vital, but unspoken, element was present in that logical matrix. It should have been spelled out in order to stand out and be reassessed, if appropriate. It was virtually the cement that lent coherence to the matrix as a whole and credibility to the related prognostication: the assumed factor of a public responsibility ethos overriding family interest in the government service. The assumption of such a factor probably underlies - yet in the end disqualifies - many a foreign prediction of 'inevitable change' in Brunei. But foreigners who have worked in the Brunei government service and found their enterprise and dedication branded as 'self-seeking', know better. We must also take into account, with special reference to the economic planners, that as Brunei bureaucrats they are not prone to identify with the present or future business class which their plans aim to foster; at least the rise of a Malay business class in Brunei is not a value taking precedence over more traditional principles such as the superiority of a career in the sultan's service and the desirability of bureaucratic rank, crowned by titles. Even less is the rise of an industrial proletariat a goal with a natural appeal, whatever the Western economic and sociological textbooks may say. The likelihood of external propaganda having any impact upon the middle bureaucratic echelons and upwards should be judged also in the light of whether the target audience is actually 'literate' in a political sense and likely to take offence at blatant political mythologising - or even be prone to perceive it as such. This is a milieu where political discourse and social analysis, never 'culturally approved', have been suffocated by a blanket of fear for a generation past; while all initiative for social action is a monopoly of the State, protected by the principle that the more radical any new policy, the more 'sensitive' it is and thus the more immune from discussion!

Concomitantly, however, Brunei bureaucratic society does not necessarily expect official declaration to represent real policy objectives. When speeches echo the doctrine currently in favour in the relevant area of activity (as all do) the demonstration effect of loyalty seems more important than follow-up. When National Day oath-takers promise to uphold Brunei democracy, there are no murmurs of derision from the grandstand.[163] In this atmosphere, again, it should not be expected that the veracity of State ideology would be subject to much critical appraisal - either its account of the present or its accounts (with their several contradictions) of the past. Indeed a certain discrepancy between 'official truth' and objective reality would be taken for granted and not arouse objections or some desire to probe the dynamics of the phenomenon. It may even be that a certain 'mystery' within and behind 'official truth' lends it an important aura of esoteric authority, of a kind once derived from the royal regalia and court Brahmins. Esoteric acumen may lend the government the desirable aura, too, of a 'modernising force', in an age of ideologies and national plans, yet without actually promoting modernity.

At all events, the Brunei bureaucratic culture is not without features related to a pre-'legal/rational' system. The reader may have spotted traces of it in earlier sections of the study. It certainly comes to mind as one gropes for a definition, if not explanation, of the 'high threshold' of critical curiosity and scepticism among educated Bruneians as they receive or, where required, help to propagate official doctrine. Islam may also play a part, since Bruneians are taught that any questioning of the truths of religion is a deadly sin. (Yet in that case how is it that Malaysian Malays are not similarly isolated from secular rationalism? The disparate historical experience of the last one hundred years, as between Brunei and the Malay Peninsula, no doubt merits careful attention - and not only with reference to the relative lack of traumatic interaction with immigrant races in Brunei. More especially one might note that the Brunei sultanate is both closely identified with religion as its protector, and simultaneously the locus of executive power. This potent combination seems to lend an unusual aura of quasi-sanctity to political authority in Brunei which its democratically based Malaysian counterpart lacks - a few desires and efforts to move the latter in the same direction notwithstanding.)

In trying to estimate or predict the impact of external propaganda, we should also ask whether our Bruneian 'target audience' is 'progressive' in the current Western mould and sets any great store by the principle of political equality which opposition tracts take as a starting point. Even if it did, another point never to be forgotten in relation to obedience to the doctrinal will of the sultan is that his absolute control of government finances makes him something more than just the head of a political structure: he is 'the boss' of the government servants, the fount of their livelihood in a peculiarly proximate way. This is not a propitious milieu for the flowering of 'middle-class conscience'.[164]

Other factors worth consideration include the enormous inequality of access to information, as between the royal family and even some of their own best-paid bureaucratic servants and advisers. The ultimate, really significant, relationships between the royal family and the world of multi-national oil corporations, could conceivably be constructed under advice from consultants who have never once set foot in Brunei. The sphere of 'defence arrangements' is not much less esoteric. But not only is the 'real' world of international oil, investment and arms deals, and the pastimes of the exceedingly rich, a closed book for educated elements in Brunei society; the latter lack even more the capacity to visualise their ruler as a man operating in two quite distinct modes simultaneously and guided in his external dealings by totally alien values. Might such values be of a kind whose mere existence the anti-Western propaganda of Brunei's official ideologues, let alone Brunei traditional culture and religion, do not begin to conceptualise? The Satan so regularly depicted from the pulpit seems to specialise in lulling Muslims into complacency about breaches of their dietary taboos, and the like: a province and level of ingenuity falling tangibly short of the specification for tutor in political legerdemain. Even cosmopolitan elements with some inkling of the international side of things may find it more comfortable to close their ears to the suggestions of rumour or intuition. But in any case it requires a considerable leap of imagination, which comes easier to devotees of academic Southeast Asian studies or students of the sociology of totalitarian political systems, to see the whole panoply of a Malay State either as a theatrical façade or as merely the power-base which delivers control of the means of production and thus true 'ruling-class' status to the fortunate incumbents. The incumbents' position is well fortified, certainly, by the common, xenophobic conviction of Brunei Malays that foreigners come to Brunei only in order to lay hands on its wealth, and - by a non-logical extension connected with faith in religious solidarity - that only foreigners

76

engage in pillage. The government need do nothing to stir up such sentiment. On the contrary it tries to dampen it somewhat in order to maintain political stability and a tolerable climate for expatriate workers.

Meanwhile, the propaganda exercise by the external secular opposition (a valuable source of thought-provoking information) looks, eighteen months later, like a 'flash in the pan', with no reinforcing sequel.[165] Also, while the ban on Arqam shows how seriously the government takes that challenge, the government's action has demonstrated a determination and capacity to retain the initiative. The fact that Arqam is seen as a threat to the established order surely reflects its nature as a rival to the government in tapping the reserves of popular allegiance to Islam which (most recently and perhaps more than anything else) the Gulf War has exposed to view. But this perspective should lead to the recognition that Islamic symbol, monopolised and well handled by the ruling elite, has an enormous potential to override critical sentiment at all levels (even among the stratum defined by 'a U.K. education'), and to preserve not only the doctrinal initiative but, most importantly, credibility in the hands of that elite. The government's rapid stock-taking and adaptation to the new situation, during and since the Gulf War, seems to indicate just such a capacity to retain the initiative as the architect of the people's perceptions by and large. The factors for political alienation which have been noted in the preceding two sections, especially among the lower-paid, are noteworthy, but need not have any decisive impact on the configuration of power. If at all, they may stimulate defensive shifts which enhance the power of the monarchy.

It seems obvious that if the royal family and its advisers, being now so well apprised of the power of Islamic appeals, subsequently see a political necessity for further Islamisation, even *at the cost* of economic development, they would not hesitate to make that choice, for self-preservation in the medium term. It would of course have to be part of the royal calculation that such a strategy would not be counterproductive as regards the loyalty of the technocrats. But there are signs that modernising elements may be willing, at a pinch, to keep a discreet silence in face of the affront to their modern principles, for similar reasons of self-preservation. This is because among the emergent skills of the ruling class must now be counted the ability to persuade the more prosperous bureaucratic echelons, through informal networks (but also by public talk of 'the priority of internal security') that, firstly, *they*, rather than the royalty, are a new class, whose assets can only be preserved from lower class envy and attack by making the masses religious; and that, secondly, inasmuch as the masses are, or are going to become, religious, it behoves any prosperous bureaucrat of prudence to adopt a more Islamic outward lifestyle himself in order to avoid popular stricture on religious grounds. The strength of Muslim feeling during the Gulf War demonstrates not only the viability of Islam as a basis for social stability under royal leadership but also, ambiguously, the potential volatility of popular emotion. Murmurs of disaffection over royal wealth, too, act as a warning signal when bureaucratic salaries are their simultaneous, if not more explicit, target; even more so where the government succeeds in 'internationalising' social envy, i.e. making the threat to internal security the more credible by suggesting that the opposition is backed by jealous foreign interests including the Western media. The vital necessity of 'a firm hand' is thus clearly indicated: action by a State of proven doctrinal acumen to ensure that Islamisation follows conservative paths, safe for private wealth under a benign royal protector and relatively lenient to more cosmopolitan private lifestyles.[166]

In other words, State ideology can be felt, by reasonably rational calculation, to offer protective advantage beyond the very narrow circle for whom it was first designed, as the subjective 'circle of privilege' expands and a sense of danger becomes more widely shared. These perceptions will be just as meaningful to those who themselves responded to the Islamic fervour of the Gulf War and experienced a 'suspension of disbelief' in relation to official ideology for that reason. Furthermore the potential efficacy of ideology is confirmed - not only for these 'believers' but even more for pragmatists - by signs that the sultan has come to believe in his own divine appointment in some degree, and will therefore be consistent both in promoting the idea itself and in adopting the more devout persona which its credibility demands. (Nor is this persona without its more 'secular' expression, in the form of a 'caring leader' image, assiduously cultivated and well calculated to efface the notion of 'the world's richest man'.)

But one privilege which, above all, the 'firm hand' will be looked to to preserve is the right to send promising offspring to the United Kingdom rather than to local institutions for pre-university and university education, helping to perpetuate the present leading families' hold on the bureaucracy into the next generation. By similar token, 'royal nationalism' in executive employment policy for Shell is an acceptable substitute for the Malay cultural identity being redefined under the second phase of M.I.B.[167]

No doubt education overseas serves more as a passport or symbol than as 'certificate of assimilation' to an alternative, 'Western' mode of thinking. Bruneians thus exposed are expected to reassure the authorities that it was possible to acquire the technology of the West without the free-thinking intellectual culture that gave rise to it (even though some of the returnees may themselves be totally 'non-M.I.B.-educated'). But few ever begin to penetrate Western intellectual culture. Their society is too geared towards continuity in its values and structure, and prone to prefer symbol to substance in matters of change, in spite of the capacity for innovation discovered at the level of exercise of power. BMWs and Mercedes cannot do more than symbolise politico-economic dynamism where the cars were bought with a government loan secured on a bureaucratic salary many years ahead and 'securing' just as much the dependence and docility of the officials concerned! Intellectual 'immobilism', expressing itself, for instance, in absence of scepticism, is a much-remarked-upon phenomenon of Brunei, already discussed in this section, which by an important paradox may be helping to guarantee the viability of ideological innovation by a class interest which itself shows many features of novelty. Inevitably 'neo-traditional' is one term that springs to mind as a key to the efficacy of Brunei State ideology or the interest promoting it. On the one hand the sense of the new is pervasive. It at least merits attention as an approach and framework for future research. On the other hand, there are several sequential ramifications to be pursued, whose ultimate outcome may resist characterisation as a 'transformation'.

Firstly, if innovation is followed and built upon by phases of further innovation (ideological renewal), combined with parallel coalition-building in response to 'environmental' challenges (whether these originate in the immediate social system or 'extra-systemically'), the demonstration effect of political versatility on the part of the 'new class' may constantly strengthen the appeal of alliance with that class against threatening formations or behaviour of more 'proletarian' aspect.[168] But thereafter, as the shared interest in the success of regime ideology grows, the actual 'veracity' of its descriptive propositions would become even less relevant to the support it receives. Nor would the regime need a society which had conformed with all these propositions in literal detail, if direct political support (as expressed by formal, symbolic faith in M.I.B.) was increasing: this means that a certain *lack* of social change would be the order of the day - yet not in mute obedience to the prescriptions of the ideology either, which strongly imply *some* change in the interests of conformity! Certainly, at the start of ideological propagation, around independence, the Brunei State seemed set to develop totalitarian pretensions as a moulder of Brunei minds and behaviour on neo-traditional lines, and such pretensions are currently more than ever active in the religious affairs ministry. Nor can the permanent political value of controlled religiosity among the less literate strata be denied. But if coalition-forming is coming to appear an attractive, feasible, and much more rapidly effective strategy, the actual behavioural demands on the 'middle class' (the middle bureaucratic echelon) in a quasi-traditional direction may prove to be moderated, even while members of this class do not hesitate to welcome and facilitate discriminatory restrictions on the lives of the lower-paid and non-Muslims.

Of course the tolerance shown towards the more cosmopolitan lifestyle of the regime's potentially key supporting stratum is conditional upon that 'Westernised' orientation remaining within limits too and not itself evincing scepticism towards State ideology or making demands for changes of behaviour at the higher social level. But such reciprocity of tolerance can be relied upon, since exemption from Islamisation must become a more valued privilege as Islamic pressures accumulate generally and turn non-conformity increasingly into a mark of royalty or those associated with royalty. In other words, self-interest in retaining a comfortable socio-economic position would be reinforced by the complementary gift of cultural autonomy. In sum, the non-transformational facets of current interactions are not necessarily, and do not indeed need to be, oriented towards literal realisation among all classes of the 'back-to-the-past' pseudo-traditionalism of M.I.B., which after the recent decades of desultory modernisation cannot have entirely static implications. But the exact and complete nature of 'non-transformation', if not a matter of fulfilling that kind of regressive ideology and giving effect to change under the guise - subtly and paradoxically - of its antithesis, still remains to be spelled out.

At this late point it might be objected, in anticipation: this use of power to manipulate ideas in defiance of the 'historical trend' in the region looks like proving the dynamism of power but not the dynamism of ideas themselves. The control of material production which possession of the State bestows is surely more important than control of the means of 'mental production'. Arguably so. But at the least, the State's relative 'monopoly of mental production' delays other ideas from coming into circulation or being assimilated and acted upon, and renders a form of negative support to continuity of control in more vital respects. (Even in Malaysia a more limited monopoly of ideas plays a part in maintaining *its* established form of political economy - yet not so visibly as in a country where school syllabuses across the board are being adapted to eliminate major inconsistency with official political doctrine.) Then, in the said context of important forms of control in Brunei other than of 'mental production', control of a loyal coalition would certainly enhance, reactively, the chances of some consolidatory social engineering along the lines implied or prescribed by doctrine itself. Conspicuous conformity in social specifics need not be expected, and is not indispensable, we have argued, but at least at the broad level of political structure, cemented by political collaboration, the myth of historical continuity and history's end, disproved at first by the *engagement* of a 'new ruling class' as such, would be set fair to work rather like a 'self-fulfilling prophecy': an independent variable guaranteeing social, economic and political stagnation far into the future.

This is the essence of the 'non-transformation' sought a few lines earlier. Manifestly, this 'consolidated stagnation' would not (unless in part through the workings of conservative Islamisation on the masses) be on a revived or neo-traditional, but on the given, *as-of-now*, basis of Brunei society. But in the latter case, as in the only slightly more dynamic former (so far as any real restoration is involved), the explanation of success would be connected precisely with the fact that the sponsors of stagnation were themselves invited by historical opportunity and environmental challenge to innovate doctrinally, adapt doctrine, and form political alliances - and proved equal to all occasions. That in general the Brunei social context proved exceptionally propitious, in its own passivity, for control of minds, would not detract from the innovating achievement. The ingenuity of the regime in also varying the blandishments towards those who prove impervious to doctrine would be an added token of 'destiny'.

Notes

1. The convention will be observed that the 'State' as a political institution is indicated by a capital S, while 'state' (lower-case s) will refer to a territorial entity enjoying international political recognition. (The fact that States in the former sense - not least the Brunei sultanate itself - may pretend that international recognition signifies approval of their political system should not cause any confusion.) The one exception to this orthographical rule is that in the phrase 'the Malay States' (of the peninsula of Malaya), the reference point is essentially territorial, despite the upper-case S.

2. The term *kedaulatan* expresses today the idea of repossession of alienated sovereign rights. For a valuable introduction to Malay politics prior to the Mahathir era, see John Funston, *Malay Politics in Malaysia. A Study of UMNO and PAS*. Kuala Lumpur, Heinemann Educational Books, 1980.

3. Dr Mahathir already enjoyed considerable intellectual influence even before becoming deputy prime minister in 1976 and prime minister in 1981. His essential pre-1969 ideas may be studied in *The Malay Dilemma* (Singapore, Donald Moore, 1970); their later development in *Menghadapi Cabaran* (Facing the Challenge); Kuala Lumpur, Pustaka Antara, 1976.

4. The neo-monarchical pretensions were visible in the political culture of the ruling party even before they were personalised by the leader: Chandra Muzaffar, *Protector?* Penang, Aliran, 1979.

5. Besides, personal dictatorship is distasteful to rivals for the Malaysian premiership! Despite symptoms of monarchical, even transcendental pretensions, it should be noted that Dr Mahathir's recurrent efforts to circumscribe royalty as such - most recently at the UMNO General Assembly, 30 November-2 December 1990 - are not yet unambiguously geared towards 'succession' to the existing royal 'protectorate' but aim rather to curb action by monarchs which is viewed as anti-democratic (i.e. anti-ruling party) by UMNO. More to the point as an illustration of absolutist pretensions (but even this depended on the cooperation of the Malaysian king) was the dismissal of the chief justice in 1988.

6. For some nuances and variations of the position that what is morally and practically unassailable nevertheless needs popular support, see Section V, including the significant title of a talk cited in note 27. See also the second paragraph of Section XI, where economic goals are seen to pose an apparent need for support *beyond* the static ideological model.

7. For suggestive approaches to questions of revolutionary elite consolidation and 'new classes' - which have not been without some influence on the

present introduction and especially the first sentence of this paragraph - see T.B. Bottomore, *Classes in Modern Society*. London, George Allen and Unwin, 1966. On a methodological point (but without wishing to engage in discussion at length): the writer is phrasing the matter in this section as if class is a given fact which can then explain particular behavioural phenomena; but what it boils down to, more exactly, is that the behavioural data listed in this paragraph are being used to propose the view that the royal family is 'a class interest', or to define it as one - a proposition which has almost certainly not been advanced before. On a comparative point, beyond the local comparison with Malaysia (but again avoiding the temptation to develop this equally fruitful dimension any further), Brunei may come to offer valuable case-study material on the totalitarian polity at a time of its general demise in Europe. Even more obviously there will be parallels between Brunei and other authoritarian Muslim states using religion for legitimation (but here too, apart from a brief commentary in note 159, the opportunity for comparative discussion is not taken up, for reasons of time and space).

8. The exceptions to this general rule were Sukarno's 'Guided Democracy' in Indonesia, the Sarit patrimony in Thailand, and Marcos's 'New Society' in the Philippines. Democratic rule was suspended in Malaysia after the 1969 riots but elections were held again within five years.

9. Cf State of Brunei, *Annual Report 1956*, p. ix: "[The party's] show of political immaturity and lack of understanding on the part of the leaders may, perhaps, be designed to enable the leaders to take credit for the outcome of the Government's development policy which must inevitably take time to reach full fruition."

10. On this period as a whole, see D.S. Ranjit Singh, *Brunei 1839-1983. The Problems of Political Survival*. Kuala Lumpur, O.U.P., 1984, Chapter 5. Brunei sent a delegation to the Federation of Malaya in 1954 to study the operation of various councils there.

11. The Constitution of the State of Brunei, 1959 (*Laws of Brunei*, S.97, 1959), Sections 24-27.

12. This is a little difficult to pin down but is inherent, *inter alia*, in Section 80 (d) of the Constitution, empowering the sultan to provide for the financial procedure of the State, and the simultaneously appearing Constitution (Financial Procedure) Order, 1959 (*Laws of Brunei*, S.101, 1959).

13. Constitution, Sections 18, 19.

14. An initial perusal of Colonial Office memoranda, etc., of the period shows up not a little concern to circumvent the monopoly of power by the royal clique, and frustration at the difficulties of the task. Whether the sultan was ever seriously attracted to British-style democracy, or skilfully negotiated time and

tide to advance dynastic interest at every turn, is a difficult but vitally important historical question. Also of critical interest is the role in the 1959 negotiations of the British Resident, Sir Dennis White, who was to be still clearly secure in the sultan's favour, as high commissioner, at the time of the rebellion and in the 1970s would be his trusted agent in the U.K. during later efforts to forestall independence and its democratic corollaries.

15. Many informative British documents on the merger proposal and Brunei's place in the scenario no doubt exist but are still subject to the 30-year rule at the time of writing.

16. That the sultan was prepared to contemplate merger with Malaysia in lieu of a separate independence, even in face of widespread popular opposition, itself suggests a strongly dynastic orientation to political development. Cf Section IX.

17. The Emergency (Suspension of Constitution) Order, 1962 (*Laws of Brunei*, S.16, 1963). See also *Laws of Brunei*, S.34, 1963, correcting the extraordinary omission of the word 'not' in the sentence "It shall not be necessary to summon the Legislative Council", in Section 2 (3) of S.16. (The basic, enabling State of Emergency, first proclaimed at the time of the rebellion - *Laws of Brunei*, E.17, 1962 - has been successively extended down to the present day.)

18. The Constitution (Amendment) Proclamation, 1964 (*Laws of Brunei*, E.4, 1964). However, the Legislative Council as such had already been reconstituted in mid-1963, with 6 *ex officio*, 10 official and 19 unofficial members: The Constitution (Amendment) Proclamation, 1963 (*Laws of Brunei*, E.2, 1963).

19. The concession was not recorded by E.4, 1964, or later.

20. The Emergency (Council of Ministers and Legislative Council) Order, 1970 (*Laws of Brunei*, S.59, 1970). For some discussion of BAKER, see Singh, *Brunei 1839-1983*, p. 210.

21. The Emergency (Constitution) (Amendment and Suspension) Order, 1984 (*Laws of Brunei*, S.8, 1984). After independence the annual Constitution Day holiday was removed from the calendar too.

22. The sultanate still claims an essentially constitutional basis, however. Apart from recurrent reference to the late sultan's 'gift of a Constitution to his people', certain policies are described as having 'Constitutional status' - as when the position of Malay as the official language was celebrated at the 30th anniversary of the Constitution in 1989, or, far more frequently (actually in a repressive spirit), when rigorous Islamisation and restrictions on other religions are justified by religious affairs officials in terms of 'the Constitutional

position of Islam as Official Religion'. Constitutionalism is invoked again, by implication (if in a spirit even further removed from foreign usage of the term), where emergency orders invoke as their authority the state of emergency proclaimed under Section 83. For instance, the order promulgating the basic statute of the University of Brunei Darussalam (UBD) is correctly cited as: 'Constitution of Brunei Darussalam (Order under Section 83): Emergency (Universiti Brunei Darussalam) Order, 1988 (*Laws of Brunei*, S.20, 1988)'. (An emergency does not, we must note, imply any urgency in matters of legislation, for the order just cited post-dates the opening of the university by three years.) Meanwhile, the PRB in exile doggedly points out that constitutional amendment was never provided as a power under Section 83, nor could any emergency order or constitutional amendment be valid without the approval of the Legislative Council (Sections 83 (7) and 85 (3) respectively). But the State now regularly passes orders to exempt itself from the latter requirement and even to maintain emergency orders in force in the event that the stipulation of revalidation of the state of emergency every two years was inadvertently overlooked. All reports of PRB statements are censored in Brunei - usually by excising a whole page of imported papers such as *The Straits Times*. For control generally, official secrecy is even more vital. (Regarding 'constitutional censorship' see note 54 below.)

23. Michael Leifer, 'Decolonisation and international status: the experience of Brunei', *International Affairs* 54 (2), Spring 1978: 240-252.

24. *Golden Silence*. London, Lonrho, 1989. This includes a Rowland letter to the prime minister, one of his most effective broadsides against his presumed rival for House of Fraser. There is ample reason to believe that the release of the last remaining 1962 detainees in January 1990, without any rituals of retraction or penitence, was urged on the sultan by the British prime minister. Above all, the effect of the Rowland publication, directly or indirectly, was to draw the sultan's attention to the fact that with the imminent release of Nelson Mandela, Brunei would soon hold a world record for longevity of political imprisonment, by succession to South Africa. It must have seemed essential to release the Brunei prisoners in advance of Mandela, in order to avoid this dubious distinction. The special irony of fearing to be pre-empted by the government of South Africa is that the Brunei government has held up South Africa to the Brunei people as an example of political evil (see Section XII). However, accommodation to the international human rights scene is a case of pragmatism, not change of values.

25. Alun Chalfont, *By God's Will. A Portrait of the Sultan of Brunei*. London, Weidenfeld and Nicholson, 1989. This is a veritable gem of 'Orientalism' but with the post-imperial variation that Brunei's simple rustics are not disturbed in the enjoyment of primordial bliss by bad Malay government; the British mission of today is thus not to intervene with reforms but to uphold

the established order, morally and militarily. The book was evidently planned some time before Lonrho's press went into top gear and may probably be seen as a pre-emptive move to James Bartholomew's anticipated *The Richest Man in the World. The Sultan of Brunei.* London, Viking, 1989.

26. See, in analytical paraphrase, Roger Kershaw, 'Illuminating the path to Independence. Political themes in *Pelita Brunei* in 1983', *Southeast Asian Affairs 1984*: 67-85. More precisely, the doctrine was first formulated as 'the Malay Islamic Sultanate'; Badaruddin's imitators later coined 'M.I.B.' The very precise synopsis of claims and aims offered in this and the following paragraph is the present writer's own. There is no official handbook. Possibly the lacuna will be made good when a national committee on M.I.B. is established (see speech by the vice chancellor of UBD, *Pelita Brunei*, 19 September 1990; this committee is to be serviced by the UBD Academy of Brunei Studies announced by the sultan on 17 July/*Pelita Brunei*, 25 July, 8 August 1990; cf note 118 below). The need for source material is pressing in view of the compulsory status of M.I.B. at UBD since 1989 and the government's intention since 1989 to include it in the school curriculum at all levels. A brief formulation from the health ministry in February 1991 does little more than to register a changing declaratory emphasis in the direction of religion: see p. 11 in the publication cited in note 163 below.

27. For one formulation of his permissive 'non-multi-racial society' concept, see Pehin Udana Khatib Ustaz Badaruddin bin Pengarah Othman, 'Seeking effective ways of integrating the Malay Islamic monarchy concept into the structure of government and State' (in Malay), lecture to university students, Part II, *Pelita Brunei*, 3 May 1989.

28. For the 'sub-group' approach, with all indigenous languages reduced to 'Malay dialects', see, from a leading light on university ideology courses, Hashim bin Abdul Hamid, 'Brunei society then and now' (in Malay), lecture notes for the M.I.B. intensive course for education ministry officials, UBD, 16-21 December 1989, p. 4. Elsewhere, however, he has argued that the non-Muslims, although defined as 'Malay' for the purpose of access to citizenship in 1961, cannot be considered full members of the national community so long as they do not embrace the dominant religion: 'A brief view on the identity of Bruneians' (in Malay), *Beriga* 2, January-March 1984: 6-10 (esp. p. 10).

29. For instance, non-Muslim indigenes are advised to classify themselves as 'free-thinkers' in national censuses, but are then taunted for having 'no religion' when applying for promotion in the government service, or for local university entrance. Warnings to non-Muslims not to 'offend' Muslim feelings are made at M.I.B. seminars but not usually in print. (Published census figures obscure the size of the remaining non-Muslim element among the indigenous; it could be 12 percent of 155,000.)

30. Hence the pregnant, if not poignant, remark by the permanent secretary for culture, youth and sports when launching a glossy periodical of his ministry: "...the Culture of Brunei...should fill every nook and void [*sic*] of our Bruneian society. To fulfill these aspirations every citizen of Brunei should love every element of the Culture of Brunei as long as it is not in transgression of [*sic*] Islam and our principles". Dato Paduka Sidek Yahya, *Warisan* 1, 1986; p. 4.

31. Haji Ahat Haji Ismail, 'Strengthen the *hadrah* as a heritage of the race' (in Malay), *Pelita Brunei*, 6 February 1991.

32. Brunei Malay society has not been able to boast of any tradition of Muslim scholarship, and even the present mufti was recruited from Johor. The Council of Religious Affairs and the foundation of a Muslim bureaucracy date back only to the last reign (1954). For an account of Brunei which classifies the state as a Muslim backwater, see Jacques Népote, 'Brunei', *Archipel* 29, 1985: 75-80. Frequent exhortation in official sermons to avoid *syirik* (polytheistic) beliefs and practices - those whose existence is hinted at in the article quoted in note 30 - strengthen the same general impression.

33. Moehammad Nazir, 'Problems and challenges facing the Bruneian identity' (in Malay), lecture notes for the M.I.B. intensive course for education ministry officials, UBD, 16-21 December 1989, pp. 32-40. In presumable reaction to Western expatriate protests at UBD against Moehammad Nazir's diatribe, the latter was given the benefit of belated weekly serialisation in the government newspaper: *Pelita Brunei*, 13 June-4 July 1990.

34. *The Independence Proclamation of Brunei Darussalam*. Strangely, however, the same sentence refers to Brunei as a democratic state: "Brunei Darussalam is and with the blessing of Allah ... shall be for ever a sovereign, democratic and independent Malay Muslim monarchy, committed to the teachings of the Sunni Sect, and based upon the principles of justice, public service and freedom." The Malay text, *Pemashshoran Kemerdekaan Brunei Darussalam*, is widely displayed in schools and government offices, as well as appearing in *Pelita Brunei*, 4 January 1984.

35. Ustaz Badaruddin, quoted in Kershaw, 'Illuminating the path', *passim*.

36. See the sultan's birthday speech from the throne, 15 August 1983: *Hasrat Negara* ('The Will of the State'). Brunei, State Secretariat, 1984, p. 4.

37. Kershaw, 'Illuminating the path', p. 76. Incidentally this assessment goes hand in hand with a taunt at Malaya for having 'allowed Britain to impose democracy' as a condition of independence in 1957. See also pp. 70, 74.

38. Partly owing to Malaysian and PRB propaganda in the 1970s, the British role was not perceived as merely 'residual'. Another influence on such perception was the presence of numerous Britons at departmental director level - in

a country a majority of whose citizens are in government employment. (On citizen employment in government, see further in note 164.)

39. Even at their level, the PRB's equation of 'independence' with 'democracy' may have coloured perceptions of events.

40. Badaruddin was moved to Indonesia as Brunei's ambassador in mid-1986, during the declining days of the Seri Begawan Sultan, and for two years after the latter's death (7 September 1986), 'M.I.B.' was little heard of. The reversion to M.I.B. and a more Islamic image for the sultanate may have been a defensive response to fundamentalism (see Section X) as well as an Islamic critique of the sultan circulated by opposition exiles. (For a discussion of other possibilities see Section XV.)

41. Singh, *Brunei 1839-1983*, pp. 108, 236. Or see a commentary on the report which led to the establishment of the Residency: M.S.H. McArthur, *Report on Brunei in 1904*. Introduced and annotated by A.V.M. Horton. Athens, Ohio; Ohio University Center for International Studies, 1987, p. 36.

42. State of Brunei, *Annual Report 1967*, p. 321.

43. *Ibid.*, p. 337. "His Highness will receive a British official ... and his advice must be taken and acted upon on all questions in Brunei, other than those affecting the Mohammedan religion, in order that a similar system may be established to that existing in other Malay States now under British protection." Brunei's paradox, clearly, was that in order to establish a 'similar system' the British took dissimilar powers.

44. Most recently, Government of Brunei Darussalam, *Brunei Darussalam 1985 and 1986*, p. 7.

45. Government of Brunei Darussalam, *Press Information*, n.d. [apparently 1989], Part I, p. 3.

46. Chalfont, *By God's Will*, p. 45. Also *Brunei Darussalam in Profile*. London, Shandwick, for the Government of Brunei Darussalam, 1988, p. 11. The latter has the courtesy to add that as the terms of the Residency did not make Brunei a colony, the other Malay States should probably not be so classified either.

47. Curriculum Development Centre, *History Teachers' Guide: Form 3*. 1986, pp. 1, 10.

48. R. Padmanabhan, *A Handbook of History for Juniors*, Vol. III. 'PSR Publishers', printed in Singapore, n.d., p. 75.

49. Hashim bin Abdul Hamid, 'The governance of Brunei: its connection with the Malay Islamic monarchy concept' (in Malay), paper presented to the International Seminar on 'Islamic Civilisation in the Malay World', Brunei, 1-5 June 1989, pp. 26a-27. (Curiously enough, the 1959 Agreement also reads

as if the high commissioner was retaining the classic power of binding advice, apart from custom and religion, but in both aim and implementation, 1959 marked a fundamental transfer of power.)

50. Hashim bin Abdul Hamid, 'Malay Islamic monarchy: a chain of continuity in Brunei culture' (in Malay), paper presented to the International Seminar on 'Language, Literature and Malay Culture', UBD, 3-8 August 1987, p. 15; and 'The Malay Islamic monarchy concept as a value system of Malay society' (in Malay), UBD Malay Islamic monarchy course prescribed text, 1989, p. 7.

51. Abdul Karim bin Abdul Rahman, 'Brunei in the 19th Century. The British challenge and intervention' (in Malay), paper presented to the Brunei History Seminar on 'Brunei in Southeast Asian Context', Brunei, 28-31 August 1989, p. 35. Independent-minded also is Minister of Religion Pehin Ratna Diraja: cf Mohamed Zain bin Serudin, 'Brunei's resilience in face of the tests of time' (in Malay), *Beriga* 18, January-March 1988: 41-45.

52. Again the present writer's translation, from *Pelita Brunei*, 4 January 1984. *Negara* does not mean 'nation', as the official translation pretends, but 'State'.

53. In a more recent presentation of Brunei's political evolution, the director of information has followed the Declaration of Independence in effectively overleaping the Residency period: see Badaruddin, 'Seeking effective ways', Part I, *Pelita Brunei*, 26 April 1989.

54. The sultan's speech to the Commonwealth heads of government in Bermuda may contain the first public declaration on the Brunei side that 'independence' was forced on Brunei against its will. (Notwithstanding its radical quality, it was translated back into Malay in *Pelita Brunei*, 23 October 1985.) This perspective may also in part clarify the Anglocentric slant of Lord Chalfont's book: on the struggle to remain under British protection, see *By God's Will*, p. 101. But a more notable monument to royal attachment to the British Empire is the Churchill Memorial in the capital. Meanwhile, to help erase the memory of the Constitution as a document of British inspiration, replete with provisions for democracy, the government published, some time after 1970, a collection of documents of the 1959 period, including a version of the Constitution itself in Jawi script, which would be assumed to be the original text but in fact gave the composition of the Legislative Council as it was in 1970 (cf note 20 above): Government of Brunei, *Surat2 Perlembagaan Negeri Brunei* ('Constitutional Documents of the State of Brunei'). N.d., p. 51.

55. See the closing lines of the previous section, and note 54.

56. There is no need to take sides on this sensitive matter, but it is difficult to deny that Brunei continued to exist only with 'colonial permission'. Cf Horton, ed., *Report on Brunei*. Corollary to this is the fact that 19th century territorial

feudalism is no kind of foundation stone or legitimating forerunner to absolutism. (The theme of 'terminal weakness' is taken up again in note 155.)

57. Mohamed Jamil al-Sufri, *Chatatan Sejarah Perwira2 dan Pembesar2 Brunei* ('Historical Notes on the Heroes and Great Men of Brunei'), Vol.II. Brunei, Dewan Bahasa dan Pustaka, 1973, p. 16. Or see his 'The story of Bendahara Sakam', *Brunei Museum Journal* 3, Part 3, 1975: 109-115. The more pedestrian facts of the matter are that the Spanish occupying force withdrew in less than three months, assailed by disease: see Robert Nicholl, 'Myth and legend in Brunei history', *Brunei Museum Journal* 6, Part I, 1985: 32-41.

58. For instance, *By God's Will*, p. 69, emphasises the allegedly external inspiration of the rebellion while the profile by Lord Chalfont's firm, *Brunei Darussalam in Profile*, p. 15, denies any local involvement at all.

59. Viz., Sultan Sharif Ali, the third sultan (and son-in-law to the second). For one of the earliest 'reconstructions' of his life, see Yura Halim, M. Jamil Umar (later Pehin Mohamed Jamil al-Sufri), *Sejarah Berunai* ('History of Brunei'). Kuala Belait, Brunei Press, 1958, pp. 21-23. Contrary to orthodox Brunei belief, his tomb seems not to be located near the Brunei capital but on Jolo in the southern Philippines.

60. Robert Nicholl, 'Some problems of Brunei chronology', *Journal of Southeast Asian Studies* 20 (2), September 1989: 175-195. (Note that the official historian usually cites 1368 as the date of conversion of Raja Alak Betatar - as opposed to his succession: cf Mohamed Jamil al-Sufri, 'Sultan Islam yang pertama' ('The first Muslim Ruler'), TV lecture, Radio-Television Brunei (RTB), 22 March 1991.)

61. This is a proposition already in conflict with the late 17th century chronicle previously recognised by the dynasty, which clearly indicates Johore: see P.M. Shariffuddin, Abdul Latif bin Ibrahim, 'The genealogical tablet (Batu Tarsilah) of the Sultans of Brunei', *Brunei Museum Journal* 3, Part 2, 1974: 253-264 (see p. 254).

62. Mohamed Jamil al-Sufri, *Chatatan Sejarah Perwira2 dan Pembesar2 Brunei*, Vol.I. Brunei, Dewan Bahasa dan Pustaka, 1971, p. 6. Or see his 'Islam in Brunei', *Brunei Museum Journal* 4, Part 1, 1977: 35-42 (see p. 38).

63. *Sejarah Melayu or Malay Annals*, Transl. C.C. Brown, intro. R. Roolvink. Kuala Lumpur, O.U.P. Reprint, 1970, p. 43. Recent excavations in Singapore have given oblique support to Malay legend by discovering evidence of a flourishing Buddhist settlement in Ming times: *The Straits Times*, 31 March 1990.

64. There has also been, recently, increasing emphasis on the claim that Islam was brought to Brunei, long in advance of the conversion of the rulers, by Arabs, not Indians or Malays - least of all by Malaccan Malays. As for the

royal conversion, according to information becoming available during 1990, a revision was in train which would see the conversion as performed not by the founder of the Malaccan Dynasty but by Sri Tri Buana's descendant who founded Malacca as such, though before his move north. However, Pehin Jamil on RTB, 22 March 1991, has presented both his earlier version (Sri Tri Buana) and a revision which yet falls short of identifying the sponsor of Alak Betatar's conversion as a Singapore ruler as late - or important - as the founder of Malacca. Since both versions were put forward in sequence without acknowledging any contradiction, it is clearly not easy to predict what the final judgement will be. But the dating of Sri Tri Buana's reign at 1299-1347 would seem to preclude him as the sponsor, at least provisionally. (Textual authority has since been released which turns out to have been the basis of the TV lecture: Muhammad [new spelling] Jamil al-Sufri, *Tarsilah Brunei* ('A Brunei Chronicle'), Vol. I. Brunei, History Centre, 1990; pp. 57-58. Ambiguity is in no way reduced by the fact that the official historian has called both possible pre-Malaccan sponsors of the Brunei conversion 'Iskandar Shah', contrary to *Sejarah Melayu*.) Meanwhile, of perhaps even greater interest to students of the 'historical imagination' is the further linkage, via Alak Betatar's mother-in-law, to a sultanate of Perlak (north Sumatra), purportedly existing already in the 9th century A.D., scarcely 200 years after Hijrah: see Mohamed Jamil al-Sufri, 'Kaitan dengan Acheh' ('The Acheh Connection'), TV lecture, RTB, 29 March 1991; also the genealogical charts at the Brunei History Centre permanent exhibition, opened in Bandar Seri Begawan on 25 February 1988. Of no less interest than the age of the Acheh monarchy is the age of Alak Betatar's mother-in-law, 'Puteri Ratna Kumala', at the time of the birth of Alak Betatar's wife-to-be: for even assuming that the latter was as old as 30 at the time of her marriage, 1368, Puteri Ratna Kumala will have been not less than 75 years old when giving birth to her daughter in 1338, since her own father, a sultan of Perlak, is said to have died in 1263.

65. "It was axiomatic that Alak Betatar had founded Brunei and forthwith had become a Muslim under the title of Sultan Muhammad, whilst all his people had similarly embraced Islam." Nicholl, 'Brunei chronology', p. 195. Foreign research which conflicts with local findings - or, as in this case, counters them with gentle ridicule - is branded as 'Orientalist distortion'. (The last speech listed in note 66 below yields an example, with implicit reference to a certain non-Bruneian interpretation of the Spanish 'defeat' in 1578: see note 57 above.) It may be noted, however, that 'revelation' can be reinterpreted by Bruneian authorities themselves, either arbitrarily (cf note 64) or when current political imperatives change. For instance, in line with efforts to strengthen the Malay identity of contemporary Brunei (i.e. in distinction to an ethnic meeting place or melting pot) the second ruler of the dynasty, Sultan Ahmad, for a few years acknowledged to have been a Chinese merchant-prince who married the first sultan's daughter (Jamil, *Chatatan Sejarah*, Vol. I, p. 9;

'Islam in Brunei', p. 38) has latterly been declared to have been the brother of the first sultan: Mohamed Jamil al-Sufri, 'Batu Tarsilah' ('The Genealogical Tablet'), TV lecture, RTB, 8 March 1991. (This lecture likewise anticipated, but was based on, Jamil, *Tarsilah Brunei*, Vol. 1. pp. 46-53.) This restores the position established in 1958 in Yura Halim, Jamil, *Sejarah Berunai*, p. 20.

66. For four clear statements of the political purpose behind research, see Badaruddin, 'Seeking effective ways', Part III, *Pelita Brunei*, 10 May 1989; Mohamed Jamil al-Sufri, 'Upholding and moulding Independence' (in Malay), *Pusaka* 1, 1988: 1-4; Pehin Laila Wijaya Abdul Aziz bin Umar, Minister of Education and UBD Vice Chancellor, announcing the setting up of a Brunei studies programme at the university, *Pelita Brunei*, 19 September 1990; and again Jamil, at the launch of *Tarsilah Brunei* on 30 May 1991 quoted in *The Borneo Bulletin*, 31 May 1991 - with a strong assertion that Bruneians are capable of self-government.

67. The sense of the 'perfection' of the present is found nowhere so strongly as in history syllabus and textbook making for secondary schools, where up-to-the-minute contemporary national history is enforced but rather in the form of a government briefing on its achievements for the people, drained of political dynamics or any element of cause and effect, let alone references to political opposition or rebellion. There is an equal absence of political dynamics in accounts of the life of the Prophet, for a slightly different reason, no doubt, yet also helping to show that, in general, evidential history does not enjoy priority.

68. Pehin Ustaz Badaruddin, address to an overseas students' long vacation civics course, *Pelita Brunei*, 16 August 1989.

69. Yusof, P.M., 'Adat Istiadat Diraja Brunei Darussalam' ('The Royal Custom of Brunei'), *Brunei Museum Journal* 3, Part 3, 1975: 43-108 (see p. 43). This is the romanised Malay text of a pamphlet in Jawi (Arabic) script first published in 1958. (Brunei authorities usually quote from the original text.) Pengiran Setia Negara Pengiran Haji Mohamed Yusof bin Pengiran Haji Abdul Rahman, as he now is, became Brunei's chief minister in the 1960s, and had, in 1951, on the eve of Sultan Omar Ali Saifuddin's Coronation, ventured into print with a romantic historical novelette about a victorious Bendahara: see, in a modern reprint, Yura Halim, *Mahkota yang Berdarah* ('The Bloody Crown'). Brunei, Dewan Bahasa dan Pustaka, 1985.

70. The following is the relevant passage from 'Adat Istiadat Diraja', p. 43 (translated rather literally): "The existence of the State of Brunei is founded on the unity and solidarity of the soul of a people who have surrendered their own individual powers to a monarch (Sultan), to be vested in the State, as its rights, on the basis that 'the Monarch may not be tyrannical' and 'the

people may not rebel against the Monarch' ... The Monarch for the People! The People for the Monarch!"

71. D.E. Brown, *Brunei. The Structure and History of a Bornean Malay Sultanate*. Brunei, The Brunei Museum, 1970.

72. Jamil, *Chatatan Sejarah*, Vol.II, p. 114. Interestingly, the code is claimed to have been seen in the hands of the same aristocrat, long deceased, who owned the 'alternative Chronicle'.

73. Brown, *Structure and History*, p. 108.

74. P.L. Amin Sweeney, ed., 'Silsilah Raja-Raja Brunei' ('The Genealogy of the Kings of Brunei'), *Journal of the Malaysian Branch of the Royal Asiatic Society (JMBRAS)* 41, Part 2, 1968: 1-82 (see p. 29). And strikingly, neither acknowledgement nor advocacy of a social contract mark a famous call to the sultanate to gird itself to face imperialism in the 1840s: Pg Shahbandar Mohamed Salleh, *Syair Rakis*, introduction by Mohamed Jamil al-Sufri. Brunei, Pusat Sejarah, 1983. An historical folktale published in Yura Halim, Jamil, *Sejarah Berunai*, pp. 63-67, relating to an early 17th century official who urged restraint and loyalty on his followers when his wife was purloined by the tyrannical Sultan Hasan, seems to convey the same general message - and this is consistent, of course, with the ideology of unquestioning loyalty promoted by all Malay sultanates throughout their history, by way of texts such as *Sejarah Melayu*. (A more 'progressive' but dubious interpretation of the latter is cited in the next paragraph.)

75. *Malay Annals*, p. 16.

76. Teuku Iskandar, 'The position of the Raja in Malay Islamic monarchy' (in Malay), lecture notes for the M.I.B. intensive course... [cf note 33], 16-21 December 1989, p. 2.

77. On the 'colonial' nature of original Malay rule in Brunei, see the 16th-century account in J.S. Carroll, 'Brunei in the Boxer Codex', *JMBRAS* 55, Part 2, 1982: 1-25 (see p. 4). Today, of course, it is the non-Muslims who have been reduced to 'enclave status': cf notes 28 and 29 above.

78. Cf the discussion in Section VII, especially paragraph 3.

79. Muhammad Hadi Abdullah, 'Sultan Haji Omar 'Ali Saifuddien: Raja yang Berjiwa Rakyat' ('Sultan Omar Ali Saifuddin. The People's Raja'), *Beriga* 30, January-March 1991: 3-24. The Arabised spelling of the late sultan's name in the title of the article was only adopted late in his life and is thus, strictly speaking, anachronistic.

80. *Ibid.*, pp. 14-18.

81. Cf the first reference in note 51.

82. *viz.*, Singh, *Brunei 1839-1983*.

83. Muhammad Hadi, 'Sultan Haji Omar 'Ali Saifuddien', p. 18.

84. Cheah Boon Kheng, 'The erosion of ideological hegemony and royal power and the rise of postwar Malay Nationalism, 1945-46', *Journal of Southeast Asian Studies* 19 (1), March 1988: 1-26.

85. *Titah 1959-67 Kebawah DYMM Paduka Seri Baginda Maulana Al-Sultan Sir Omar Ali Saifuddin Sa'adul Khairi Waddin*. Brunei, Dewan Bahasa dan Pustaka, 1971, p. 156.

86. Muhammad Hadi, p. 16, quoting from *Titah 1959-67*, pp. 167-168.

87. Pehin Datu Seri Maharaja Ismail bin Omar Abdul Aziz, 'The basic principles of the Sunni Sect in State Administration' (in Malay), in *Aqidah Ahli Sunnah Wal-Jamaah* ('The Faith of the Sunni Sect'), Vol. I. Brunei, Pusat Dakwah Islamiah, 1986, pp. 30-31. See also Mohamed Zain bin Serudin, 'Hadiths of Government: obedience and loyalty' (in Malay), *Mimbar Hadith* ('The Hadith Pulpit'), Vol.I. Brunei, Department of Religious Affairs, 1972, pp. 36-37. And note the weekly sermon on the occasion of the sultan's 43rd birthday, 'Obedience to the monarch is a duty' (in Malay), *Pelita Brunei*, 19 July 1989; and on his 44th, 'Obedience to the Head of State is a binding religious responsibility' (in Malay), *Pelita Brunei*, 18 July 1990.

88. On the prevalence of this orthodoxy throughout the Malay world, see Mohamed Nor bin Ngah, *Kitab Jawi. Islamic Thought of the Muslim Malay Scholars*. Singapore, ISEAS, 1982, pp. 40-44.

89. Mohamed Zain bin Serudin, 'Islamic civilisation in the Malay World: a general perspective' (in Malay), keynote address to the international seminar on 'Islamic Civilisation in the Malay World', Brunei, 1-5 June 1989, p. 25.

90. Abdul Aziz bin Umar, opening the M.I.B. course referred to in notes 33 and 76: *Pelita Brunei*, 10 January 1990.

91. Mohamed Zain bin Serudin, at the national Koran Reading Contest, 30 January 1990 (*Pelita Brunei*, 21 February 1990).

92. In this way, in fact, absolutism may seem reconcilable with an idea of 'contract', as in the quasi-'Hobbesian' surrender of popular rights cited in note 70 above.

93. The caliph takes advice, but is not judged on earth: Mohamed Zain, *ibid.*, and Maghfur Usman, 'Government in Islam' (in Malay), lecture notes for the course on 'Islam as a way of life', UBD, 1990, pp. 10, 17. (Maghfur does speak of retribution for bad rule occurring on earth as well as in heaven, but it is clear that such punishment is not administered by mortal men. Maghfur even admits that there may be disputes regarding the nature of 'just rule'

(p. 12) but instead of attempting a definition in political terms, simply states that such uncertainties may be resolved by reference to *syariah*: everything that is compatible with it is *ipso facto* just.) For a naive or disingenuous account of 'Malay, Islamic monarchy' - Divine Right tempered by social concern - packaged for the British audience, see Chalfont, *By God's Will*, pp. 14, 15, 177. But for a Bruneian account of the blessings (and implied personal legitimacy) which flow from the mere fact of the royal Haj, see Pehin Tuan Imam Abdul Aziz Junid (deputy mufti), *Menjadi Tetamu Allah* ('Guest of God'). Brunei, Ministry of Education (repr.), 1990, pp. 137-139. (While a corps of local luminaries stand ready to design and develop the sultan's religious profile, several of the university lecturers involved in indoctrination - including Maghfur and Moehammad Nazir - are not in fact Bruneian.)

94. For a clear indication of this comity of interest, see the stirring last part of a serialised fatwa (theological dictum of the mufti), Ismail bin Omar Abdul Aziz, 'Bringing up children in the Islamic way' (in Malay), *Pelita Brunei*, 25 January 1989, in which he calls for institutions of Islamic education throughout Southeast Asia, among whose goals would be to lay the groundwork for a restoration of the (by implication, absolute) power of monarchs.

95. Cf the speech of the sultan at the Feast of Israk Mekraj (the Ascension), on 12 February 1991 (*Pelita Brunei*, 20 February 1991); and the sermon by Pehin Khatib Haji Awang Abdul Wahid bin Haji Awang Besar at the State Mosque on Friday 15 March 1991 (text in *Pelita Brunei*, 20 March 1991). Clearly for both the sultan and the religious establishment the most alarming facet of Arqam is the 'competitive' heresy that locates charisma on earth in the awaited Second Coming of 'Al-Imam Al-Mahdi Al-Muntazar'.

96. In an outstanding political sermon at *Hari Raya Haji* (Feast of Pilgrims) on 4 July 1990, Pehin Ustaz Badaruddin explicitly rationalised Brunei's commitment to Islam under the sultan's leadership as a way of pre-empting deviant religious activity. But fortunately, also, Brunei had not 'lost its way' in the first place because of colonialism, so there is no need for religious radicalism. The privilege of delivering the *Hari Raya Haji* sermon, however much politicised, falls to Pehin Badaruddin not as a permanent secretary in the government but as holder of the religious office of *Udana Khatib*; still, this fusing of clerical and political roles (like the rise of a 'charismatic sultan') is strangely suggestive of the Shi'a tendency which the sermon was designed to depreciate (if the sermon was not designed to conjure the spectre of Shi'aism in order to justify the consolidation of the power of a Sunni establishment). For full text, see *Pelita Brunei*, 11 July 1990. That Badaruddin was 'rehabilitated' after a period on the sidelines, in late 1988, was noted in note 40. Another important restoration of late 1988 was that of Pehin Abdul Aziz as minister of education and UBD vice chancellor. He is not religious-trained

but enjoys a strongly religious reputation. (For an introduction to the Sunni-Shi'a division in Islamic history, and the incompatibility of 'constitutionalism' with 'charisma', see W. Montgomery Watt, *Islamic Political Thought*. Edinburgh, Edinburgh University Press, 1968.)

97. Texts which evince the radical new suppression of the Malay dimension of M.I.B., or its assimilation to Islam, include the Maulud (Prophet's Birthday) speeches of the deputy mufti, Pehin Abdul Aziz bin Junid, and of the sultan for Hijrah 1411 (see *Pelita Brunei*, 10 October and 17 October 1990, respectively). The former quotes the Prophet's dictum that racial consciousness is natural but must cede to Islam; the latter identifies correct Malay behaviour completely with Islamic morality. This has very serious implications for the lifestyle of Malays as well as the prospects for moving Malay culture in the direction of greater economic dynamism, but foreshadows far worse pressures on non-Muslim indigenous culture, now on the verge of exclusion from any definition of 'Malay' (see Section V above) and prone to be branded as 'non-national' if not 'anti-national'.

98. A strong case against female employment has been made by Dr Haji Abdul Aziz bin Haji Hanaf, 'The Islamic view on women and wives working outside the home' (in Malay), *Pelita Brunei*, 5, 12, 19 June 1991.

99. Speech to an ASEAN heads of government meeting in Manila. *Pelita Brunei*, 23 December 1987.

100. *Pelita Brunei*, 17 June 1987.

101. National Day Supplement to *Pelita Brunei*, 24 February 1988.

102. Requoted in *Pelita Brunei*, 6 September 1989.

103. *Pelita Brunei*, 19 July 1989.

104. *Pelita Brunei*, 4 March 1987.

105. *Pelita Brunei*, 30 August 1989.

106. *Pelita Brunei*, 25 April 1990.

107. The sultan, quoted in *Pelita Brunei*, 19 July 1989, 30 August 1989. Pengiran Isteri Mariam (the sultan's second wife), opening a new secondary school, quoted in *Pelita Brunei*, 21 December 1988.

108. The sultan, speaking just after the arrest of certain party politicians and the banning of their party. *Pelita Brunei*, 24 February 1988.

109. The minister of education and vice chancellor launched the university in 1985 with a speech which equated academic freedom with student riots, and on these terms seemed to rule out academic freedom for the new institution. See summary in *Pelita Brunei*, 30 October 1985.

110. See Royal Birthday Supplement, *Pelita Brunei*, 15 July 1987.

111. It is unthinkable, for instance, that even an environmental society devoted to saving Brunei's disappearing sandstone hills from the developers would ever receive a permit under the state of emergency.

112. *Hasrat Negara*. Brunei, Government of Brunei Darussalam, 1988, p. 30.

113. See Badaruddin, 'Seeking effective ways', Part II, *Pelita Brunei*, 3 May 1989, on Brunei as a non-multi-racial society. For an example of policy implementation, see Minister of Education Pehin Abdul Aziz on the decision to impose, in line with policy for government schools, a Malay-medium curriculum on the first three years of private primary education (i.e. including Chinese schools), reported in *Pelita Brunei*, 20 June 1990.

114. The speech from the throne at the royal birthday in 1990, and official commentaries when military hardware is shown on TV or in parades, have left no doubt that internal security is the more important concern of the security-cum-defence forces. *Pelita Brunei*, 18 July 1990.

115. *Pelita Brunei*, 13 June 1990.

116. *Pelita Brunei*, 21 February 1990.

117. Badaruddin, 'Seeking effective ways', Part III, *Pelita Brunei*, 10 May 1989. The growing tendency of government officials by 1991 to treat M.I.B. as 'state policy' was noted at the end of note 67.

118. The sultan at his 1990 birthday audience in Belait; *Pelita Brunei*, 8 August 1990. Again, however, the workings and fruits of Providence need to be demonstrated: the sultan also said that responsibility for research on M.I.B. would be vested in a special academy at UBD. *Ibid.* (A later, and stronger, assertion that Brunei's monarchical rule is specifically willed by Allah was made by the sultan at Prophet's Birthday. *Pelita Brunei*, 17 October 1990.)

119. Mastura Hj Mohiddin, *Pelita Brunei*, 11 July 1990. The letter is full of English loan words which lend a touch of would-be modernity and dynamism. This includes the last word of all, *progresif.* Grasping and rendering the exact connotation of new loan words is among the more difficult aspects of translation. It may not be wrong to suggest that lack of precision makes them usefully ambiguous in a context devoted precisely to the reconciliation of contradictory objectives.

120. *Viz.* in the last sentence of the penultimate paragraph of Section V, relating to Moehammad Nazir, 'Problems and challenges'.

121. *Ibid.* See the section published in *Pelita Brunei*, 13 June 1990.

122. Speech at the National Koran Reading Contest on 14 January 1991. Full text in *Pelita Brunei*, 23 January 1991; summarised in *Brunei Darussalam Newsletter*, 15 February 1991. While the former gave headline prominence to the sultan's call to all Muslims to develop the skill of Koran reading, the summary in the English newsletter, which circulates mainly to foreign missions, was headed "'Give Darussalam own image and identity as a non-secular country' - HM Sultan to his people."

123. Cf Mohammed Zain, 'Islamic Civilisation', pp. 10-15; and Moehammad Nazir, 'Problems and challenges', in the section published in *Pelita Brunei*, 4 July 1990.

124. Mohammed Zain, 'Islamic Civilisation', p. 8. And the Hari Raya Haji sermon by Pehin Ustaz Badaruddin, 16 August 1986 (unpublished), another piece of outstanding oratory from the *Udana Khatib*, rare for its fire in present-day Brunei. (On the actual cause of the Spanish retreat in 1578, see note 57 above.)

125. Ismail bin Omar Abdul Aziz, 'Mixing with non-Muslims' [but differently headed in subsequent weeks] (in Malay), fatwa, *Pelita Brunei*, 10, 17, 24 and 31 October 1984. A report of less than total reverence in *The Borneo Bulletin*, 3 November 1984, provoked a further and much more extensive judgement, viz. Ismail bin Omar Abdul Aziz, *The ruling of Syara' on the Free Masonry Organisation and the ruling on clubs under the Free Masons, with the ruling on membership of the Free Masons and their clubs, and on 'Borneo Bulletin' and the Mufti's tract* (in Malay), Fatwa No. 55. Office of the Mufti, Department of Religious Affairs, Brunei, 19 March 1985 (mimeo., 87 pp.). See p. 20 of the later fatwa on the 'Protocols of the Elders of Zion'. The Zionist conspiracy and Free Masonry are also dealt with by Moehammad Nazir, 'Problems and challenges', but merely echoing the mufti: see *Pelita Brunei*, 20 June 1990, for the relevant section. (This UBD lecturer has also followed a fatwa - the one cited in note 94 above - in the section of his paper on Western education, reprinted on 13 June 1990.)

126. Mohamed Zain, 'Islamic Civilisation', p. 26. For further reference on the rebellion see note 58 above.

127. See the speech by the sultan at the United Nations General Assembly in 1984, upon Brunei's accession to the organisation, in *Kemasukan Negara Brunei Darussalam ke Pertubuhan Bangsa-Bangsa Bersatu* ('The Entry of Brunei Darussalam to the United Nations'). Brunei, Information Department, 1984, pp. 14-26.

128. A commentary on the Gurkha Battalion in an edition of Brunei Television's *Liputan Nasional* ('National Round-up'), 13 April 1988, covering a visit by the sultan to a Gurkha training area, merely skirted the boundary of diplomatic impropriety in suggesting that the Gurkhas' high state of professionalism

should be an example to '*all* [the rest of?] His Majesty's forces'; but a similar exposé on the renamed *Liputan Semasa* ('Topical Round-up'), 21 June 1991, crossed the boundary with a bold opening statement (in Malay) that: "although ours is a small country ... the area of security [*keselamatan*] is given constant attention. In this connection, in the quest to upgrade the performance of all army personnel even more, military exercises are frequently held, both inside the country and abroad. And today, in a jungle location in Labi, Belait District, the Second Battalion, King Edward's Own Gurkha Rifles, held an ... exercise."

129. *Kemasukan Brunei Darussalam*, pp. 19, 21.

130. With reference to Michael Leifer's framework of 1978 - see the article quoted in note 23 above - the logic of the Brunei government's defence would have to be that an indigenous ruling elite satisfies the criteria of international legitimacy.

131. See the account of this episode in note 24.

132. Readers will excuse this pun on the sultan's excursion into personal foreign policy in 1986, suggestive of an emotional alignment with the United States as well as Britain, when he made a handsome donation to the Nicaraguan opposition at the urging of Secretary of State Shultz.

133. Cf articles from the Malay language newspaper most widely read in Brunei, *Berita Harian*, such as Kassim Ahmad, 'America's real motive is imperial power' (2 November 1990).

134. Ignatius Stephen, 'The great Gulf bluff', *The Borneo Bulletin*, 5-6 January 1991. The interest in this newspaper on the part of Prince Mohamed (the sultan's first younger brother, Perdana Wazir and foreign minister), since the recent takeover by his company, has never been a secret.

135. Printed belatedly in *Pelita Brunei*, 28 November 1990.

136. Mohammed Salleh Abdul Latif, 'The United Nations Organisation is increasingly effective' (in Malay), *Ibid.*

137. Mohammed Salleh Abdul Latif, 'Intifadah, the spirit of Palestinian struggle, so gentle in tone yet capable of shaking the Tel Aviv regime' (in Malay) *Pelita Brunei*, 19 December 1990.

138. The sultan's speech appears in *Pelita Brunei*, 2 January 1991. Some Brunei intelligentsia read a deeper meaning into the sultan's words than a plea for loyalty: they thought that the sultan was assuring the people that he himself, unlike the emir of Kuwait, would remain loyal and never run away.

139. Awangku Badaruddin bin Pengiran Yaakub writes the English television news bulletin of RTB twice or three times a week, in harness with one other

member of the news department. Usually this script is used as the basis for the Malay language bulletin which follows, with a few 'voice-over' additions in lieu of foreign agency sound where the latter had been allowed in the English bulletin. Awangku Badaruddin seems to have fulfilled in highest degree the guidelines of Brunei's chief theorist of the media, Dato Haji Abu Bakar bin Apong (now vice chancellor of UBD) in terms of the creative adaptation of Western reporting to 'Bruneian aspirations': cf speech by Dato Abu Bakar to a Regional Seminar on TV writing and editing, *Pelita Brunei*, 13 March 1991.

140. See MFA statements in *Pelita Brunei*, 23 January 1991, 27 February 1991. Indeed the foreign minister in his 3 October 1990 speech at the United Nations had declared that the real cause of conflict in the Middle East was Israeli aggression: *Pelita Brunei*, 28 November 1990.

141. Ignatius Stephen, 'Back to the stone age', *The Borneo Bulletin*, 9-10 February 1991.

142. Ignatius Stephen, 'Chasing an elusive dream', *The Borneo Bulletin*, 30-31 March 1991, tells the life story of a campaigner for the restoration of Limbang.

143. Haji Ahmad Awang, 'The most horrible example of a tyranny against Islam' (in Malay), *Watan*, 28 February 1989.

144. Lance Morrow, 'Evil', *Time*, 10 June 1991, pp. 40-45.

145. C. Mary Turnbull, *A Short History of Malaysia, Singapore and Brunei*. 2nd edition. Sydney, Allen & Unwin, 1989, p. 295.

146. The best-seller in Bandar Seri Begawan bookshops - one Indian Muslim bookseller, who anticipated and seized the opportunity as the war broke out, achieved a turnover of 2,000 copies within a fortnight, retailing at B$6.90 each - was a collection of militant essays by 19 different authors: Shoutul Islam, *Perang Salib di Teluk Parsi. Saddam bela Islam* ('Crusade in the Persian Gulf. Saddam defends Islam'). Kuala Lumpur, Penerbitan Hikmah, 1991.

147. Full text in *Pelita Brunei*, 27 February 1991.

148. *Ibid.*

149. *Pelita Brunei*, 6 March 1991.

150. Cf 'The role of our country in settling issues of the Islamic world' (in Malay), editorial, *Pelita Brunei*, 15 August 1990.

151. By Abdul Aziz bin Junid, deputy mufti, in the Omar Ali Saifuddien Mosque on 24 May 1991.

152. The sultan's TV address at the Feast of Pilgrims, 23 June 1991.

153. By Chief Kathi Pehin Datu Imam Dato Paduka Seri Setia Haji Abdul Hamid bin Bakal, in the Sultan Omar Ali Saifuddien Mosque on 7 June 1991. Quite radical by Brunei standards was the warning that God will punish those who fail to support the Palestinian struggle. See *Pelita Brunei*, 3 July 1991.

154. See references in note 37 above.

155. Regarding discontinuity - of power if not, ultimately, succession - and the willingness to cover it up in official chronicles, see Nicholl, 'Brunei chronology', pp. 191-192, describing for the first time 'the Great Void' in the 18th-century part of the royal genealogy. It is also notable that the Brunei government completely ignored the Limbang centenary on 17 March 1990. It would appear that even a discontinuity which can be justly blamed on others is too much at variance with the main ideological line to be given publicity. It is more compatible with present imperatives to celebrate a Gurkha Centenary and stress the past and present viability of the Anglo-Bruneian connection (see *Pelita Brunei*, 9 May 1990) than to draw attention to historic disasters.

156. Cf Lord Chalfont's alternative, astonishing suggestion, likewise designed to project the private-public dichotomy, that the wealth of the Brunei royal family is an accumulation of centuries: *By God's Will*, pp. 147-148. Interestingly, Lord Chalfont does see fit to merge the public and private sphere when justifying the size of the palace on the grounds of its simultaneous use as the seat of the administration (*loc. cit.*).

157. As in the 1991 National Day slogan, 'Through unity consolidate national resilience!'

158. Speech from the throne, 1990. *Pelita Brunei*, 18 July 1990. 'Malay triology' (anon.), a quite well-informed piece in *Far Eastern Economic Review*, 15 November 1990, goes so far as to attribute ideological propagation first and foremost to government anxiety about youth unemployment and consequent social problems; avoidance of democratisation is seen only as a supplementary or secondary benefit of M.I.B. (particularly its Islamic aspect). What in fact is most interesting about the article is that the edition of *FEER* containing it was passed for sale in Brunei unexcised, contrary to usual practice in cases of analytical reporting of the country. It is possible that the home affairs minister saw value in the article as a signal of reassurance to secular-minded elements that Islamisation is merely instrumental - a means to quite separate ends which a broad spectrum can embrace. Yet one notes that ideology is cast as a substitute for economic development, not as its guarantee.

159. For reference to the sultan as a protector of his people from the ills of modernisation, see *By God's Will*, Chapter 9 (e.g. pp. 190-191). The pervasive untruth in the Chalfont account is its suggestion that the sultan's conservative strategies, including Islamisation, are designed to protect the people, whereas, rather patently, Brunei reveals certain similarities with other Muslim states

where ruling interests protect *themselves* by resort to religious symbol. However, the sultan of Brunei has been relatively free to choose his own timing. The embryonic Al-Arqam, to which the government has responded with incremental Islamisation, arose to make an Islamic critique of the sultan's politics; it was not a classic nativist movement seeking to protect a cultural tradition from erosion.

160. Under such a game-plan the 'fundamentalist danger' would figure as not much more than the pretext whereby the planners convinced the religious interests, through the sultan, that their motive in supporting Islamisation was 'honourable', but the subtlety of the strategy does not detract from its potentially counterproductive nature. The planners may also in the end have to face up to a contradiction between anti-Chinese employment policy (backed by many other pressures for emigration - cf note 113) and the need for Chinese qualifications, skills and applications in industry.

161. A Malay version of the publication cited in note 24 above was the most numerous item in the mass distribution of January 1990. The sultan had however already pre-empted some of its criticism by releasing the last of the 1962-period rebels.

162. *The Straits Times*, 14 April 1990. Or see Party Rakyat Brunei, *The Third Manifesto*. Kuala Lumpur, 1990, p. 1.

163. Cf the text in *Sambutan Hari Kebangsaan Negara Brunei Darussalam kali ketujuh. 1991.* Brunei, Programme Book and Printing Committee for the Seventh Anniversary of Brunei Darussalam's National Day, 23 February 1991, p. 9. The reference to democracy echoes, of course, the Declaration of Independence: see note 34 above.

164. Not only does the sultan employ 'the middle class': he also employs, directly or indirectly (through Shell and Royal Brunei Airlines), a large part of the salaried/wage-earning population.

165. It is difficult to assess whether the sermon by Pehin Khatib Haji Ahmad bin Abdul Razak at the State Mosque on 9 August 1991 (see *Pelita Brunei*, 14 August 1991), with its interesting warnings of infidel slanders (designed to divide Muslims like the 'current deceitful peace efforts' in the Middle East) was a reaction to a renewed propaganda initiative by the opposition, or an attempt to pre-empt unsavoury fall-out from Lonrho's suit against a British ex-minister - or just any future agitation.

166. Illustrating the new 'social volatility', the media now focus on the phenomenon of burglary by locals, where a few years ago crime was always attributed to immigrant workers; and the ban on alcohol imports since the beginning of 1991 is justified rather more as a safeguard for social order, by keeping youths off drink, than as a step in Islamisation (though not excluding this). That

youths are now turning more to drugs is an ironical but not necessarily dysfunctional effect of the new rigour.

167. It should be pointed out that the 'bureaucratic elite' in its present composition bears witness to a fair degree of 'sponsored' social mobility in the recent past. (Cf Timothy Ong Teck Mong, 'Modern Brunei: some important issues', *Southeast Asian Affairs 1983*: 71-84.) The fact that bureaucratic position was recently gained does not however lessen the urge to see one's heirs similarly endowed; nor reduce a sense of obligation to the monarchy for present benefits, in the light, for instance, of policies of discrimination against 'permanent residents' (i.e. young Chinese whose parents for some reason 'missed the boat' of citizenship before Independence), for the private sector. The political advantage of this policy outweighs the loss to industrialisation noted in note 160.

168. Versatility helps to confirm, analytically, the notion of a 'new' ruling class; but in real terms it is also an asset in the search for perpetuation, less likely to be found in a highly institutionalised environment.

List of Principal Works Cited

Bottomore, T.B. *Classes in Modern Society*. London, George Allen and Unwin, 1966.

Brown, D.E. *Brunei. The Structure and History of a Bornean Malay Sultanate*. Brunei, The Brunei Museum, 1970.

Chalfont, Alun. *By God's Will. A Portrait of the Sultan of Brunei*. London, Weidenfeld and Nicholson, 1989.

Chandra Muzaffar. *Protector?* Penang, Aliran, 1979.

Funston, John. *Malay Politics in Malaysia. A Study of UMNO and PAS*. Kuala Lumpur, Heinemann Educational Books, 1980.

Golden Silence. London, Lonrho, 1989.

Mahathir Mohamed. *The Malay Dilemma*. Singapore, Donald Moore, 1970. (Or, in Malay translation, *Dilema Melayu*. Kuala Lumpur, Federal Publications, 1982.)

Mahathir Mohamed. *Menghadapi Cabaran*. Kuala Lumpur, Pustaka Antara, 1976. (Or, in English translation, *The Challenge*. Petaling Jaya, Pelandok Publications, 1986.)

McArthur, M.S.H. *Report on Brunei in 1904*. Introduced and annotated by A.V.M. Horton. Athens, Ohio, Ohio Center for International Studies, 1987.

Mohamed Nor bin Ngah. *Kitab Jawi. Islamic Thought of the Muslim Malay Scholars*. Singapore, ISEAS, 1982.

Muhammad Jamil al-Sufri. *Tarsilah Brunei. I. Sejarah Awal dan Perkembangan Islam*. Brunei, History Centre, 1990.

Sejarah Melayu or Malay Annals. Translated by C.C. Brown, introduced by R. Roolvink. Kuala Lumpur, O.U.P. Reprint, 1970.

Shoutul Islam. *Perang Salib di Teluk Parsi. Saddam bela Islam*. Kuala Lumpur, Penerbitan Hikmah, 1991.

Singh, Ranjit D.S. *Brunei 1839-1983. The Problems of Political Survival*. Kuala Lumpur, O.U.P., 1984.

Watt, W. Montgomery. *Islamic Political Thought*. Edinburgh, Edinburgh University Press, 1968.